Disc One

Disc Two

GRAHAM NASH

AND

MANUSCRIPT ORIGINALS

PRESENT

Songwriters on Songwriting

*25 of the
World's Most Celebrated Songs*

Introduction and CD Narration by Graham Nash

**Andrews McMeel
Publishing**

Kansas City

Credits

Produced by Michael James Jackson

Art direction, design, and co-editing by Junie Osaki

CD produced and audio interviews conducted by Adam Mitchell

Text interviews conducted by Steve Salzburg

Music renditions by C.J. Vanston and Brian Adler

Additional guitar by Billy Panda

Project administration by Mary Ellen Buckley

Photo research by Wendy Heller-Stein

Legal services provided by Scott Brisbin

Executive assistant: Jan James

Mac Holbert by Mac Holbert

Music clearance consultant: Chad Jensen, All Clear

Business consultant: Marc Firestone

Business consultant: Joe Patterson

Accounting services provided by Grant, Tani, Barash & Altman

"Still rocking his ass off" by Graham Nash

Acknowledgments

We would like to thank Junie Osaki for her extraordinary talent, dedication, and brilliant design; Mary Ellen Buckley, without whose remarkable organizational skills and diligence this book could never have been constructed; Adam Mitchell for his dedication, talent, and wonderfully conscientious work; Steven Salzburg for his good help; Wendy Heller-Stein for her excellence ("thank you"); Mac Holbert for his skillful artistry and support; Jan James for her executive assistance; C. J. Vanston for the music; Chris Schillig for her patience and good counsel; Marc Firestone for his support and bringing us to Andrews McMeel Publishing; Joe Patterson for his wise and invaluable counsel; Graham Howe for his support; Kelly Jackson for adding a very good idea; Scott Brisbin; Kathleen Stewart; Susan Nash; Paul Whitteker; Chad Jensen; Tom Thornton; Hugh Andrews; Lance Freed; Julie McDowell; Jerry Davis; Anna Davis; Zakiya Hooker-Bell; Linda Taylor; Trish Farrell; Bonnie Raitt; Kathy Kane; Doreen Ringer-Ross; Gail Agcaoili; Carolyn Jones; Mary Ann Bastian; Teressa Rowell; Barbara Cane; Lorna Guess and Sharon Thompson at CK Music; Jane Tani; Michael Weston; Stacey Gordon; Fred Walecki; Mark Bookin; Bill Long; Lisa Silbar; David Rudich; Jay Morganstern, for whose continuing support of Manuscript Originals we will always be grateful; all of our friends at Nash Editions; Billy Panda; Gigi Causey; Michael Jensen; Nikki Mitchell; Jessi Colter; Lisa Davis; Claire Weiss; Greg Bechtloff; Cheryl Beychok; Su Brazie; Leslie Douglas; Richard Ackerknecht; Todd Ellis; Jan Hightower; Christy Ikner; Glen Friedman; Kathy Spanberger; Kathleen Carey; Jody Graham-Dunitz; Don Biederman; Jack Rosner; Mike Kappus; Steve Lee; David Earl Jay; Jeannie Johnson; Wendy Leshner; Jeffrey Molina; Gregory Nagy; Browndog; Jesse Snyder; Marc Zubatkin; Michael Cohl; Murray Lester; Ken Lester; all of the Manuscript Originals artists; the Manuscript Originals Board of Advisors (Chuck Kaye, Rupert Perry, David Anderle, Lenny Waronker, Hale Milgrim, Barry Ollman, Brenda Andrews, and Bob Ezrin) for their support; and to each of the twenty-five participating artists in this book, which by its very limitation can only honor a small portion of their gifted talent, we thank you.

02 03 04 05 06 QGR 10 9 8 7 6 5 4 3 2 1

Library of Congress Cataloging-in-Publication Data on file.

Manuscript Originals® is a registered trademark.

Emmy® ATAS/NATAS

GRAMMY® NARAS

Billboard Chart references are copyrighted and the use is granted by the owner, VNU Business Media, Inc.

BMI performance plays and the BMI Top 100 Songs courtesy of BMI. Founded in 1940, BMI is an American performing rights organization that represents approximately 300,000 songwriters, composers, and music publishers in all genres of music. Through its music performance and reciprocal agreements with sister organizations around the world, it grants businesses and media access to its repertoire of approximately 4.5 million songs and compositions.

Attention: Schools and Businesses

Andrews McMeel books are available at quantity discounts with bulk purchase for educational, business, or sales promotional use. For information, please write to: Special Sales Department, Andrews McMeel Publishing, 4520 Main Street, Kansas City, Missouri 64111.

About This Book

Music and song have likely been an intrinsic part of every culture in the world since the beginning of time. Even in ancient Greece, before alphabetic writing was used to record literature, Homer's *Iliad* and *Odyssey* were not only spoken as tales but also sung, frequently accompanied by music that was considered a part of the basic form of storytelling. In our own time and culture, there is no question that music is the dominant art form.

Off the Record makes no pretense to be the definitive book on songwriting. Its intent is to celebrate songwriters and the powerful role the art of songwriting plays in our lives. The twenty-five songwriters who appear in this book, each of whose own catalogue of work far exceeds their one song shown here, represent a broad cross-section of styles, genres, backgrounds, and creative perspectives. There are literally thousands of classic songs that have profoundly impacted our lives, brought us comfort, and put us in contact with the deepest part of ourselves. This book of twenty-five songs is able to commemorate but a few of them. In spirit, it pays homage to them all.

Several years ago, I had the privilege of spending some time with the legendary John Lee Hooker. As his manager and I entered his home, John Lee was seated on his couch, wearing his trademark hat, completely entranced by a football game. The purpose of our meeting was to discuss Manuscript Originals and to have John Lee hand-draw his lyrics for us. I sat down and introduced myself and, at first, got no response. John Lee just continued to watch the TV. A long, awkward moment passed in silence. I looked to the manager in confusion. Was John Lee Hooker unaware of the reason I was there? Suddenly, without ever taking his eyes off the TV, John Lee asked me in that unmistakable voice of his, "Do you love what you do?" Neither the question itself nor an answer would have occurred to me. I'd been a record producer for over twenty-five years, and initially I had thought I would simply help Graham put Manuscript Originals in motion and then return to my own pursuits. But John Lee's question was so succinct, so direct, it made me realize that Graham's concept for this company honored the very thing that had caused me to remain in the music business so many years myself—the impact that great songs always had on me. Consequently, it wasn't hard to look back at him and honestly say, "Yes, I do." Then and only then did John Lee finally turn to me, smile broadly, and say, "That's good. It's good to love what you do." I doubt he would have talked to anyone who didn't.

John Lee Hooker's measuring stick for what is important in life goes to the heart of this book about great songs and the songwriters who created them. It's about having a passion for what you do, for the process, and for the elegant mystery that always accompanies the creative effort.

The text interview portion of this book is intended to give the reader a sense of each writer's background and his or her personal journey through a life of music and songwriting. Most of these twenty-five songs were cowritten with other equally talented songwriters, whose contribution we wish to acknowledge, for without their collaboration these classic songs would never have existed.

The audio interview portion of this book on the enclosed CDs is intended to provide a firsthand account of the genesis of a particular song by one of its writers. Out of necessity, these audio interviews were conducted through a variety of means, ranging from in-person interviews, whenever possible, to remote recording devices, phone lines, and archived materials. Although the quality of these recordings may vary from interview to interview, we felt that by their very nature, their character and color added greatly to a sense of the individual and the process of songwriting.

Manuscript Originals was created in 1993 by Graham Nash and several music industry associates to honor and commemorate the classic songs of our times in the form of museum-quality, limited-edition handwritten lyrics rendered by one of the song's original composers. These limited-edition pieces are available through the Neiman Marcus stores, art galleries, and other exclusive venues throughout the country.

Michael James Jackson, President, Manuscript Originals

Contents

Introduction

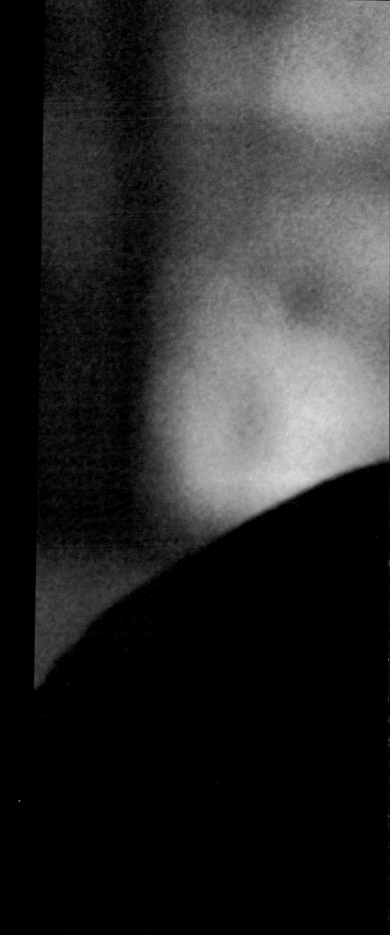

In 1992, I was asked to donate a personal item for an auction that was being held by a local school near my home in the Hawaiian Islands to raise funds for the school's athletic gear that was destroyed by the ravages of Hurricane Iniki. I had a photograph of my friend, Joni Mitchell, which I had taken some years before. I thought it would be a good choice. In an effort to make it a little more special, I thought I'd handwrite the lyrics to the chorus of my song "Our House" around the margin of the photograph.

On the night of the auction, I was very pleased to watch this piece raise several thousand dollars for the children at the school. Afterward, I approached the woman who had purchased the piece and told her I was genuinely over-whelmed she would pay so much for the photo with the chorus of my song on it. She smiled and said, "Mr. Nash, you make a mistake. You may think this is your song, but this is really my song. Years ago, my boyfriend put this song on the turntable, dropped down on one knee, and then proposed to me. Now I have a piece of that song and a moment that I'll cherish forever."

This incident was instrumental to the inception of our company, Manuscript Originals. It so clearly and simply illustrated to me that music truly touches more than just people's hearts; it affects our lives in ways that are indescribable. I am still amazed by the intensity of feelings that get stirred up in me when I hear the music I grew up with. So many of the key moments in my life have songs that serve as their emotional landmarks. My recollections of becoming a young man are flooded with the colors and the music of those years. I've always felt the same is true for all of us.

Songwriting has always been one of the most effective ways I communicate. There've been plenty of times when I've been asked about my songs and someone will say, "How did you write that?" And quite honestly, I never really have any idea. All I know is that songs are the most powerful tools imaginable and they serve to bring us all to a place where we can experience shared memories and emotions. Manuscript Originals was established to celebrate the work of great songwriters throughout the world and to honor classic songs that continue to endure throughout time.

Graham Nash

Disc One
Track 2

Richard Addrisi on
"Never My Love"

Never My Love
Don and Dick Addrisi

You ask me if there'll come a time
when I grow tired of you

Never My Love, Never My Love

You wonder if this heart of mine
will lose its desire for you

Never My Love, Never My Love

What makes you think love will end
when you know that my whole life
depends . . . on you?

You say you fear I'll change my mind,
I won't require you

Never My Love, Never My Love

How can you think love will end
when I've asked you to spend
your whole life with me?

Never My Love, Never My Love

Chapter 1

Richard Addrisi

PHOTO: DAVID HUDGINS

The Addrisi Brothers

"Never My Love"

You ask me if they'll come a time
　　when I grow tired of you
　　　　Never My Love
　　　　Never My Love

You wonder if this heart of mine
　　will lose its desire for you
　　　　Never My Love
　　　　Never My Love

What makes you think love
　　will end
　　when you know that my whole life
　　depends on you

You say you fear I'll change my mind
　　I won't require you
　　　　Never My Love
　　　　Never My Love

How can you think love will end
when I've asked you to spend
your whole life with me.

　　　　Never My Love
　　　　Never My Love

Dick
&
Don
Addrisi

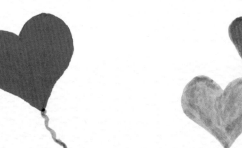

"In the thirty-two years since 'Never My Love,'
what has lasted? Has the Association lasted?
Has the Fifth Dimension lasted? It's the song
that lasted; it's a song that will always live on."

"I can remember having to fly in from Las Vegas to pick up my high school diploma, then getting right back on the airplane to catch the last show."

The Association

PHOTO: PAUL RYAN/MICHAEL OCHS ARCHIVES.COM

"Never My Love," written by Richard and Don Addrisi, was recorded by the Association for Warner Bros. Records in 1967. Climbing Billboard's Hot 100 for eleven weeks, it reached the #2 position and earned a gold record. The Fifth Dimension stayed nine weeks on the top forty charts with their cover of the song in 1971. It has since become the second most performed song in BMI history, with over eight million broadcast performances. Don Addrisi passed away in Los Angeles, California, in November of 1984 and is survived by his two daughters, Alexis and Amity. Richard Addrisi currently divides his time between Nashville, Tennessee, and Los Angeles, California.

Both my brother, Donald, and I were born in Winthrop, Massachusetts. Don was born in 1938 and I was born in 1941. My mom and dad were the Flying Addrisis, a trapeze act. They ended up in Boston, which worked out to our advantage because Boston was a music town. My brother started out by himself, doing tap and singing, you know, the usual stuff that kids do, except he was extraordinary at it. One night, as he was doing his show, I kind of jumped in and got some laughs myself. From that moment on, I knew that was where I wanted to be.

Do you think songwriting is more a matter of inspiration or just plain hard work?

For me, inspiration always comes first and then I think you have to sit down, focus, and not get up until the song is written. You just can't leave the room until the song is finished. So it's more like half and half.

What does it take to put you in the mood to write?

It depends on where you are and, sometimes, who it is you're working for. At a publishing company, you would have had "writers' rooms." You'd go in there at about ten o'clock in the morning and you'd stay in that little room until the job was done. If I'm writing for myself then I work from inspiration and that can come anywhere, anytime.

What's your favorite distraction that can get you out of the mood to write faster than anything else?

A pretty girl.

What kind of music were you listening to early on?

Back in those days we listened to the music they played on a program called *Your Hit Parade*. I don't want to date myself here, but they played all kinds of music from Rosemary Clooney and Nat King Cole and who was that Italian kid from Philadelphia? I'll think of his name in a minute, but anyway, it was the music of that era.

What kind of material did you and your brother perform at that time?

They'd be the current songs of the day [sings], "Maybe you'll think of me, bee bum, bum . . ." all those songs that made it out of vaudeville. In 1950 or so there was a radio show called *The Original Amateur Hour* that my brother had been on and won. When we got our act together as a duo, we went back on the show. By then, it had made its move to television.

Was it important to become successful for anyone else other than yourself?

In the early stages, it was my mother and father. Around 1950, my mom, dad, my brother, and I took our first trip by car out to the West Coast. My parents had bought a brand-new Studebaker that had no radio. You might ask, "Why no radio?" It was so we would sing and harmonize. My mother would teach us different harmonies all the whole way across the country, and so that's why no radio. My father was a Shriner and a member of the Elks Club. So the first thing he did when we pulled into Chicago was give a call to the Elks Club and find out if they had some function or other coming up that weekend. When they'd say, "Yes," he'd say, "Well, I've got two sons who sing and we'd love to do the show." So we'd go to the Elks Club that Saturday night and do the show. We had these little straw hats we'd pass around at the end of the show and people would throw money in the hats. It wasn't enough money to survive on; it was just that my folks felt it was good practice for us and it paid. We made that trip across the country two or three times like that. The second time we came to Los Angeles, we went to a place that showcased new talent that was run by Red Skelton, Red Buttons, and Milton Berle. One night after we had finished our act, this guy came up to us and said, "You kids are good!" He introduced himself and said his name was Lenny Bruce. This was long before Lenny was known as a "dirty" comic. My mom and

Donald and Richard Addrisi
Palm Springs, 1975

PHOTO: ED CARAEFF

7

dad told him we had to go back East at the end of the summer to finish school. He said if he heard of anything that was right for us he'd give us a call. It wasn't until June of the following year that we finally got a call from Lenny. He said they were holding auditions for a new show with Disney called *The Mickey Mouse Club*. So we got back in the car for our third trip to the coast and tried out for the Mouseketeers. After the audition, we were told that we were great but the problem was, we were too professional. They wanted kids who were talented, sure, but no one was to be any more talented than anyone else in the group. We looked like we had been performing all our lives, which was not far from the truth. They told us they were working on a series called *Spin and Marty*, which they thought we'd be better suited for, and so my brother and I worked on that show for a while. This was about when my father decided to move the family permanently out to the West Coast. We moved to Studio City and started working on our career. It's so funny to think of Lenny Bruce and the Mouseketeers in the same breath, when most people think of him as a foul-mouthed, trouble-making nightclub stand-up. I saw him again probably about a year before the end. I said, "Lenny, how's things going?" He said, "Well, you know, in the old days when I didn't do smut, I think I had more fun. You know kids, we could have gone on to do this and do that…" But his career took a different road.

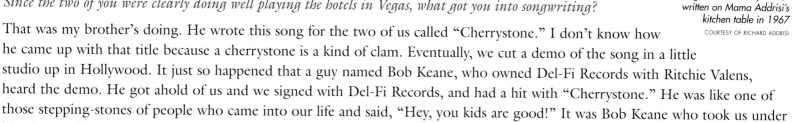

The original "Never My Love,"
written on Mama Addrisi's
kitchen table in 1967
COURTESY OF RICHARD ADDRISI

When did you and your brother start to think you might have made it?

It goes back to our roots in Boston. There was a guy by the name of George Clarke who was a columnist for a daily paper that's now known as the *Boston Herald*. He took a liking to us as young kids and made sure we were always booked on the big shows that Sinatra and Peggy Lee used to do. As a result of those shows, we became quite well known on the East Coast. Later on, we gained some notoriety by being the youngest act to work Las Vegas. I was thirteen and Don was, I think, fifteen. We worked at the Hacienda Hotel, at the Dunes, the Sands Hotel, the Flamingo, all up and down the strip.

You guys must have had to grow up pretty fast.

We really did. I can remember having to fly in from Las Vegas to pick up my high school diploma and then get right back on the airplane to catch the last show.

Since the two of you were clearly doing well playing the hotels in Vegas, what got you into songwriting?

That was my brother's doing. He wrote this song for the two of us called "Cherrystone." I don't know how he came up with that title because a cherrystone is a kind of clam. Eventually, we cut a demo of the song in a little studio up in Hollywood. It just so happened that a guy named Bob Keane, who owned Del-Fi Records with Ritchie Valens, heard the demo. He got ahold of us and we signed with Del-Fi Records, and had a hit with "Cherrystone." He was like one of those stepping-stones of people who came into our life and said, "Hey, you kids are good!" It was Bob Keane who took us under his wing and brought us into the realm of the record business.

What was it like hearing yourself on the radio for the first time?

We had done a record called "We've Got to Get It on Again" for Columbia Records. One day, my brother and I went to the beach and were lying in the sand. This was when KHJ was the biggest radio station around L.A., and on this particular day, we just happened to be lying near these two beautiful blondes when we heard our song come on the radio. It was almost like hearing it in stereo as it played off all the radios on the beach, from down to the pier on the left and all the way on the right to

Malibu. You couldn't hear anything but [sings], "We've got to get it on again." So I turned to Don and said, "Don, this is my shot." I got up and walked over to where this gorgeous blonde was lying in the sun, stood by her feet, and said, "That's my brother and me on the radio, the Addrisi Brothers [sings], 'Got to get it on again.'" There was a beat and then she said to me, "You're in my sun." It was the perfect introduction to "Show Business 101."

Is there anyone in show business that you wish you could have sat down and talked to?

I think that it would have been Nat King Cole. Nat King Cole was extremely important to my brother and me. We used to go down to my mom and dad's garage and be tinkering around with the radio on. We just sat there and listened to those vocal parts of Nat Cole's and listened and soaked in things that we used ourselves later on.

Has anyone ever stood in your way or tried to talk you into doing something else?

Nobody really stood in our way because we weren't exactly around the "B" or "C" team. If you put yourself with the "A" team, you can become an "A" player. You stick around with the "B" team and you're a "B" player. Unless you can see that in your career, you'll be stuck working with talent that isn't as talented as you are.

Has there ever been any misconception about the Addrisi Brothers that you'd like to set straight?

We really took our music very seriously. But some people thought our success never reached the point of really breaking open, and I suppose that was probably due to the fact that we chose not to go on the road. I'm sure our decision about that was a holdover from having been on the road our whole lives, so that by the time we had achieved some success within the record industry, the idea of touring again was just too much. What we did instead was to do shows like *The Merv Griffin Show* and *The Dick Clark Show*. We did a lot of interview shows and tried to keep the business going that way. I also think it proved to be right for us because when the Association went out on the road, they stopped writing. When the Fifth Dimension went out on the road, they stopped writing. Don and I just kept on writing. I mean, in the thirty-two years since "Never My Love," what has lasted? Has the Association lasted? Has the Fifth Dimension lasted? It's the song that lasted; it's a song that will always live on.

Donald and Richard Addrisi performing at the Ritchie Valens Memorial Dance and Show at the El Monte Legion Stadium in 1959. (Ritchie Valens is shown in the framed photograph onstage.)

Disc One
Track 3

Randy Bachman on
"American Woman"

American Woman

Burton Cummings, Randy Bachman, Garry Petersen, and Jim Kale

American Woman, stay away from me
American Woman, mama let me be.
Don't come here hangin' around my door,
I don't want to see your face no more,
I got more important things to do
Than spend my time growin' old with you.
Now Woman, I said stay away
American Woman, listen what I say.

American Woman, get away from me
American Woman, mama let me be.
Don't come knockin' around my door
Don't wanna to see your shadow no more
Colored lights can hypnotize
Sparkle someone else's eyes
Now woman, I said get away
American Woman, listen what I say.

American Woman, said get away
American Woman, listen what I say
Don't come here hangin' around my door
Don't wanna see your face no more
I don't need your war machines
I don't need your ghetto scenes
Colored lights can hypnotize
Sparkle someone else's eyes
Now woman, get away from me
American Woman, mama let me be
Go, gotta get away, gotta get away, now go go go,
I'm gonna leave you, woman, gonna leave you woman.
Bye bye, Bye bye, Bye bye.

You're no good for me, I'm no good for you.
Gonna look you right in the eye, tell you what I'm gonna do.
You know I'm gonna leave, you know I'm gonna go.
You know I'm gonna leave, you know I'm gonna go, woman.
I'm gonna leave, woman, goodbye, American Woman.
Goodbye, American chick, goodbye, American broad.

Chapter 2

Randy Bachman

AMERICAN WOMAN stay away from me american woman mama let me be don't come hangin around my door i don't wanna see your face no more i got more important things to do than spendin' my time growin old with you now woman said stay away american woman listen what i say AMERICAN WOMAN get away from me american woman mama let me be don't come knockin around my door don't wanna see your shadow no more coloured lights can hypnotise sparkle someone else's eyes now woman said get away american woman listen what i say AMERICAN WOMAN said get away american woman listen what i say don't come hangin round my door don't wanna see your face no more i don't need your war machines i don't need your ghetto scenes coloured lights can hypnotise sparkle someone else's eyes now woman get away from me american woman mama let me be go gotta get away gotta get away now go go go i'm gonna leave you woman bye bye bye bye bye you're no good for me i'm no good for you gonna look you right in the eye tell you what i'm gonna do gonna leave you know i'm gonna go you know i'm gonna leave you know i'm gonna go goodbye american woman goodbye american chick goodbye american woman goodbye bye bye ★burton cummings·randy backman·jim kale·garry peterson★

Randy Bachman 03 April 02

"I . . . saw Elvis on The Ed Sullivan Show and said, 'What is that?' I was told it was called rock and roll. I had been so restricted playing classical violin that all I wanted was to do something so wild, so abandoned, something like Elvis was doing right there on The Ed Sullivan Show."

"So when people ask me, 'What would you do if you weren't a successful rock musician?' I always say, 'I would be an unsuccessful rock musician.'"

The Guess Who

"American Woman," written by Randy Bachman, Burton Cummings, Garry Peterson, and Jim Kale was recorded by the Guess Who for RCA Records in 1970. Released on Valentine's Day, it held the #1 position for three weeks on Billboard's Hot 100 *and earned the group a gold record. Lenny Kravitz later recorded the song and won a Grammy Award in 1999 for Best Male Rock Vocal Performance. The Guess Who was honored in 2001 with a star on the Canadian Walk of Fame in Toronto, Canada. Randy Bachman currently lives near Victoria, British Columbia.*

I was born in the forties in Winnipeg, Manitoba, which may be a relatively small prairie town but out of it has come the Guess Who, Bachman Turner Overdrive, Neil Young, Loreena McKinnett, and the Crash Test Dummies, to name just a few. There's just something about that place. Maybe it's the six or seven months of winter snow or the thirty or forty degrees below zero winters. You're ten, eleven, twelve, thirteen, whatever, and if you don't play hockey, then you stay indoors in the winter, which made for an incredibly embryonic situation for guys to get together and jam, form bands, and develop a style of music. Winnipeg is like a small New York. There's a Polish section, a Jewish section, an Irish section, a British section—little boroughs of ethnic groups. Growing up, we were influenced by what was played at the weddings, the parties, stuff like that. Every band out of Winnipeg was totally different from every other band. Being so isolated and not really having TV at that time, I listened to AM radio from the States—stations broadcasting out of Chicago, Oklahoma City, and New Orleans. We'd always get the best stuff late at night when that signal could bounce around all the way to Winnipeg and we even got Wolf Man Jack once in awhile. The beginning of so many bands there was listening to those stations and dreaming about rock and roll; that was the genesis.

Would you say songwriting is 99 percent inspiration and 1 percent perspiration or maybe the other way around?

Well, each song is different. I think that most songwriters will tell you that some magical thing can happen and then a song just drops in your lap—that all you have to do is wake up and basically write out two-thirds or more of a song. You say to yourself,

"Wow, this is incredible." Then you ask people, "So have you ever heard this anywhere before?" When they say, "No," you just say, "Well, I guess I wrote it after all and maybe the angel of songwriters dropped it in my lap." Other times it's an assignment like, "I need another song to complete my album." A slow song, a fast song, a love song, a driving song, a dance song—that's where the perspiration comes in, because you've got to sit there and hammer away until you come up with something. After awhile you learn to adapt to all these environments, writing with someone else, writing by yourself, being totally inspired by another song, a movie, a book, life. And then there's also the drudgery of saying to yourself, "I haven't written a song in three weeks." Every single day and every single song is different.

Does inspiration come easy to you?

The simple answer is sometimes I chase a song and sometimes it chases me.

Do you think first in words or music?

I'm basically a music guy. I've always had melodies in my head. I've been told my guitar solos are very melodic and that singers can sing them and that's probably because I started out with the violin. Basically, what I bring to a session with other artists are chord progressions and riffs and melody lines.

Was there someone along the way that you wanted to prove yourself to?

I was very influenced by a guitar player named Lenny Breau. He was about a year older than I was. I was fifteen and he was just sixteen. He had been playing in this family band since he was about six and had mastered that Chet Atkins/Merle Travis finger style. He was the first guy I hung out with musically. I absorbed a lot of technique from him and then I got into more rock and roll with music like Elvis, Scotty Moore, and Gene Vincent, that kind of thing. Lenny got more into jazz. Then there was also this scruffy kind of guy who was always at my gigs talking about the guitars and amps, and that was Neil Young. In those days everyone was so poor, and I guess that's just the only word for it,

PHOTO: HANS SIPMA

that there'd only be one or two amplifiers in the whole town. So if we ever had a day off, Neil would call up and say, "Could I borrow your amp?" And we'd say, "Sure." So before he could take a gig, he'd always have to call and see if he could borrow the amp and sometimes a bass. We had the only Fender Precision Bass in town.

What was the first real taste of success that you can remember?

Early on, we weren't writing great original material and we knew it. It seemed like every time we would do a cover of some "oldie," it would come out first from a British band. The Beatles were doing "Dizzy Miss Lizzie" and "Slow Down," and the Searchers were doing "Needles and Pins." I had a cousin living in London who would send us her old singles at the end of every year. One of the singles she sent was "Shakin' All Over" by Johnny Kidd and the Pirates. She said it had been number one in the U.K. in 1960 or 1961 but by now, it was '63 or '64, I'm not quite sure. So we covered it and sent it into our label and they said, "Wow, this sounds like a British record. We're going to release it but we're not going to put your name on it. We don't want anyone to know you're a Canadian band from Winnipeg. So we're going to put 'Guess Who' on the label and then they all can guess who it is. Then we're going to start little rumors like 'Hey, it's a guy from the Stones' or 'It's someone from the Yardbirds,' or 'It's Jeff Beck on guitar.'" Then they released the single. The record had a white label on it that had "Shakin' All Over" written on it in about one-inch block letters. At the bottom it just said "Guess Who" and a question mark. That song went to number one in Canada.

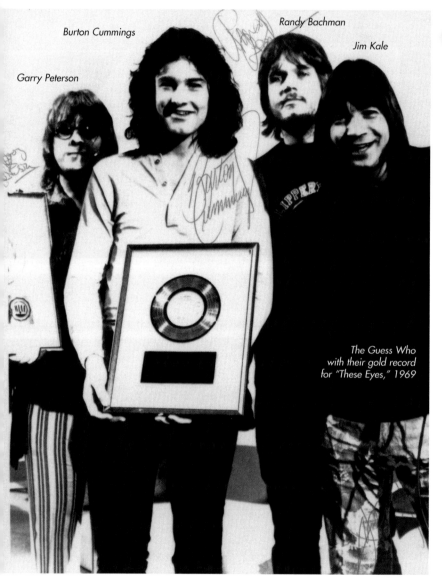

Garry Peterson

Burton Cummings

Randy Bachman

Jim Kale

The Guess Who
with their gold record
for "These Eyes," 1969

So the marketing guys picked the group's name?

That's how it happened. Then the song got picked up by Scepter Records in the States and went top twenty while I was still in high school. I couldn't afford *Billboard* magazine, so I'd take the bus every Saturday to a record store where they sold *Billboard* to see how high the record had climbed on the charts. Otherwise, we'd have had no idea. About then we got a call from Paul Cantor, who managed Dionne Warwick and the Kingsmen, who were on Scepter's sister label. He called to say that the Kingsmen wanted us to do a summer tour with them and we said, "Wow, the group that recorded 'Louie, Louie!'" We went to New York to meet with Cantor and to work out the details. That's when we met Dionne Warwick, Burt Bacharach, and Ashford and Simpson. That incredible summer of '65 we toured with the Kingsmen. So there we were, doing the Dick Clark caravan bus tour thing that we had seen in movies and on television and still barely out of high school. While we were in New York we got our first and last royalty check for four hundred dollars. We said, "Wow, a hundred bucks each, isn't this incredible?" That was our first big taste of success.

How did you celebrate?

Well, it wasn't much of a celebration but we were in New York when we got the check and since we were going on tour, we went out and bought suitcases. I got one of these black airline travel-ons that you put in the overhead. I still have it. My daughter uses it; she loves it.

Any heroes you would like to have spent some time with?

Yes, Elvis. I played classical violin from the age of five till fourteen. I found it so restrictive having to play these old notes written by dead guys hundreds of years ago, so I just stopped playing. Eventually, someone got the first television in our neighborhood—a little twelve-inch black-and-white TV. After school we'd go over just to watch this magical thing in the living room. We watched *Howdy Doody, Range Rider*, things like that. Then one day, I got invited over on a Sunday night and saw Elvis on *The Ed Sullivan Show* and said, "What is that?" I was told it was called rock and roll. I had been so restricted playing classical violin that all I wanted was to do something so wild, so abandoned, something like Elvis was doing right there on *The Ed Sullivan*

Show. My cousin had a guitar that I could borrow, and after he showed me three chords, I took it home for a week. By the time I returned it, I could play better than he could due to the very classical training I had found so restrictive. Basically, I could play any lead line I heard and so I started to play Scotty Moore. It was also about then that I met Lenny Breau who took me all through the Chet Atkins, Merle Travis styles, et cetera. Once I could do the country finger-picking thing with coordination, then the Chuck Berry, Duane Eddy styles came very easily to me. But in the beginning, it was all Elvis. Decades later I heard that Elvis had taken my song title, "Takin' Care of Business" as his personal motto. Supposedly he had heard it on the radio in L.A.

while going to the airport in his limo and said, "Crank that up. I love that song. That's going to be my motto—TCB with a lightning bolt." Priscilla Presley told the story on a TV program while giving a tour of Graceland. I was pretty thrilled because it was Elvis who first introduced me to rock and roll and the wild abandon of doing whatever you want on your instrument and people going crazy to it. When the group [the Guess Who] was breaking up in the late '70s, an invite came to go see Elvis in Las Vegas, but they never told me about it and they went without me. I found out after the fact that they had met Elvis, who was my reason to get in the business in the first place. The TCB logo and the lightning bolt are on his tombstone.

Anyone ever try and dissuade you from doing music?

My high school principal, Ronald Reginald Bailey, or as he signed his name, R. Squared Bailey, took me and Garry Peterson, the drummer for the Guess Who, aside and said, "You guys gotta forget this rock and roll nonsense. You need to stay in school and get a real job." Needless to say the advice fell on deaf ears. Some thirty years later we got inducted into the Walk of Fame in Toronto and were given an honorary doctorate by the University of Manitoba and there sitting in the front row in tears was R. Squared Bailey. Afterwards he came backstage and said, "Boy, just think, if you guys had listened to me, you wouldn't be where you are today." Basically, I believe I was born with a gift for music. So when people ask me, "What would you do if you weren't a successful rock musician?" I always say, "I would be an unsuccessful rock musician."

Randy Bachman and his son Tal in Randy's home studio, Winnepeg, 1970

Disc One
Track 4

L. Russell Brown on
"Tie a Yellow Ribbon Round the Ole Oak Tree"

Tie a Yellow Ribbon Round the Ole Oak Tree
Irwin Levine and L. Russell Brown

I'm comin' home, I've done my time,
Now I've got to know what is and isn't mine.
If you received my letter tellin' you I'd soon be free,
Then you know just what to do if you still want me,
If you still want me.

Tie a yellow ribbon round the ole oak tree,
It's been three long years, do ya still want me?
If I don't see a ribbon round the ole oak tree
I'll stay on the bus, forget about us, put the blame on me,
If I don't see a yellow ribbon round the ole oak tree.

Bus driver please look for me,
'Cause I couldn't bear to see what I might see.
I'm really still in prison and my love she holds the key,
Simple yellow ribbon's what I need to set me free,
I wrote and told her please.

Tie a yellow ribbon round the ole oak tree,
It's been three long years, do ya still want me?
If I don't see a ribbon round the ole oak tree
I'll stay on the bus, forget about us, put the blame on me,
If I don't see a yellow ribbon round the ole oak tree.

Now the whole damn bus is cheering and I can't believe I see
A hundred yellow ribbons round the ole oak tree.

Chapter 3

L. Russell Brown

TIE A YELLOW RIBBON ROUND THE OLE OAK TREE

I'M COMIN HOME I'VE DONE MY TIME NOW I'VE GOT
TO KNOW WHAT IS AND ISN'T MINE IF YOU RECEIVED MY
LETTER TELLIN YOU I'D SOON BE FREE THEN YOU'LL
KNOW JUST WHAT TO DO IF YOU STILL WANT ME
IF YOU STILL WANT ME

    TIE A YELLOW RIBBON ROUND THE OLE OAK TREE
IT'S BEEN THREE LONG YEARS DO YOU STILL WANT ME
IF I DON'T SEE A RIBBON ROUND THE OLE OAK TREE
I'LL STAY ON THE BUS FORGET ABOUT US PUT THE BLAME ON ME
IF I DON'T SEE A YELLOW RIBBON ROUND THE OLE OAK TREE

BUS DRIVER PLEASE LOOK FOR ME CAUSE I COULDNT
BEAR TO SEE WHAT I MIGHT SEE I'M REALLY STILL IN PRISON
AND MY LOVE SHE HOLDS THE KEY A SIMPLE YELLOW RIBBONS
WHAT I NEED TO SET ME FREE
I WROTE AND TOLD HER PLEASE

    TIE A YELLOW RIBBON ROUND THE OLE OAK TREE
IT'S BEEN THREE LONG YEARS DO YOU STILL WANT ME
IF I DON'T SEE A RIBBON ROUND THE OLE OAK TREE
I'LL STAY ON THE BUS FORGET ABOUT US
PUT THE BLAME ON ME IF I DON'T SEE A
YELLOW RIBBON ROUND THE OLE OAK TREE

NOW THE WHOLE DAMN BUS IS CHEERIN
AND I CANT BELIEVE I SEE A HUNDRED
YELLOW RIBBONS ROUND THE OLE OAK TREE

Russell Brown

"All I've ever done was try to write songs to entertain people, give them a few brief moments of musical relief, something to remove them from the world for a moment and their everyday problems. Above all, I've just wanted to entertain."

"So then John Lennon gets me in a headlock and starts laughing and punching me saying, 'That bloody, son-of-a-bitch song of yours. They just won't stop playing that bloody song. I can't stand it.'"

Dawn
Tony Orlando, Telma Hopkins,
and Joyce Vincent

PHOTO: MICHAEL OCHS ARCHIVES.COM

"Tie a Yellow Ribbon Round the Ole Oak Tree," written by L. Russell Brown and Irwin Levine, was recorded by Dawn (Tony Orlando, Telma Hopkins, and Joyce Vincent) for Bell Records in 1973. It debuted on Billboard's Hot 100 *in March of that year and remained there for seventeen weeks, four of which it held the #1 spot. It received the Most Performed Song of the Year Award from BMI in 1974 and was nominated for a Grammy Award for Song of the Year. The* Guinness Book of World Records *recognized it in 1974 for being the second most recorded song of all time. "Tie a Yellow Ribbon" became an anthem for the returning Vietnam vets and then again for the hostages during the 444-day Iranian Hostage Crisis. L. Russell Brown currently lives in Nashville, Tennessee.*

I was born in Newark, New Jersey, on June 29, 1940. Some people might think it was a misfortune to be born in the housing projects of Newark among hundreds and hundreds of families of every different persuasion. Some people might also think it a difficult thing to have been the only white boy in my high school class. But as I look back, I realize that I couldn't have learned what I did in a more homogenous or parochial society. Living among people of every color and persuasion forced me to learn how to get along. I was exposed to so many cultural and musical influences at such a young age. What also had an effect on me was that my father was an amateur singer and played Bing Crosby, Al Jolson, and Nat King Cole around the clock in the house.

Were those your original musical influences?

I always loved to listen to Patti Page sing "Old Cape Cod," loved that kind of music from the late forties. But the thing that had the most impact on me and blew my mind as a kid was when a friend of mine played me a 78 record by this guy named Elvis Presley singing "That's All Right, Mama." I heard the record before his first TV appearance on the *Stage Show* hosted by the Dorsey Brothers and it had a strange impact on me; I can't really explain it. It was like seeing the messiah, musically. When I saw Elvis, I got it right from the start. I said to myself, "That's what I want to write, that's what I want to be." It was an incredible kind of exciting sound, with an echo and a rhythm to it that got to me. So I borrowed a friend's guitar and in ten days I learned how to play it note for note. Two weeks later I started making records. At the age of sixteen I was rejected by every record company in New York City until I ended up in Harlem with a guy named Bobby Robinson. Bobby Robinson owned a black label called Fury Records where Wilbert Harrison had his hit with "Kansas City." So my first record with the Duals was released on Fury Records.

Do you consider songwriting to be more a matter of hard work or inspiration?

Let me explain it to you this way: I've always had a hard time trying to sit down and write a song. Of the over two thousand songs I've written, the ones that are really successful songs are the ones I didn't "write." You know what I'm saying by that? Here's a perfect example and it's a weird thing. I had a colonoscopy eight months ago and they put me under with a general anesthetic to do it. I woke up an hour later in recovery when the nurse and the doctor came over to me and said, "You sat bolt upright in the middle of your colonoscopy and said something." Now they were both laughing at me, so I said, "Okay, so what did I say?" The doctor said that what came out was, "Sometimes I get some of my best ideas in the middle of the night and then I get up and write them down on a piece of paper." I think that says it all. Sometimes the words come first; sometimes the melody. But there's no set form. I don't ever sit down and just try and come up with a new idea.

Do you have a set routine or place that puts you in a creative mood?

The last song I wrote, I wrote in the shower. I don't know how it just came to me, but it did. It can happen in a car, anywhere. I've written a song while I was stuck in the Lincoln Tunnel. Whenever the "Boss" gives me the message that's when I write it down.

Was there anyone early on in your life that you wanted to prove yourself to, or succeed for?

I suppose the person I really wanted to prove myself to was myself. I met my wife when she was sixteen years old, and I married her when she was twenty. We've been together now for thirty-seven years. Most every song I've ever written, I wrote for her.

When was the first time you realized you had broken through with your songwriting?

It was very strange how it happened so quickly. My mentor and teacher, the man who taught me everything I know about songwriting and the music industry, was a fellow named Bob Crewe. Bob Crewe created the Four Seasons and produced all their hits. He also produced Oliver and wrote "Can't Take My Eyes Off of You," "Lady Marmalade," and so many more, a true genius. Crewe signed me in 1964 and made me write two songs a day for five straight years. At the end of each day he would cut my attempts to ribbons until I was near tears. Halfway through our time together, he and I wrote a song for Mitch Ryder called, "Sock It to Me Baby" which was a million-seller. That was how it all started, and it was my first taste of success. I was signed as an artist and our group was called the Distant Cousins. Bob Crewe produced us, me and my partner, Raymond Bloodworth. We had a record that was in the top ten in twenty markets and then we got on the Dick Clark tour. I felt

L. Russell Brown and his wife, Lisa

successful, but I really didn't make much money. The following year I wrote "C'mon Marianne" and just to show you how bizarre the business is I wrote that song on a Wednesday, Bob Crewe heard it on Thursday, and the Four Seasons agreed to do it on a Friday. They recorded it over the weekend and the acetate [record] was brought to WABC, WINS, and MCA on Monday afternoon. By the end of that day, it was the Pick of the Week on every station. By Tuesday it was a monster hit and it wasn't even a week old! It all happened that fast, and just as fast, it was also the end of my career as a performing artist.

You mean your success as a writer derailed your plans of being a performer?

Precisely. I had written songs so I could sing them. I wanted to be a performer. But not long after I had written "Knock Three Times," I walked out of my house, looked around, and said to myself, "Brown, you're a songwriter."

Was there any time you doubted your work?

I'll give you the classic, the quintessential answer. I wrote a song called "Tie a Yellow Ribbon Round the Ole Oak Tree" with Irwin Levine. We decided to bring it to Apple Records to play it for Ringo Starr. So we went and met with the head of A&R [artists and repertoire] for the company, a man named Al Steckler. We got out the guitar and attempted to sing the song live. When we got to the chorus, Mr. Steckler grabbed the guitar neck, deadening the strings, looked at me, and said, "This is embarrassing. You've had hits before but this song could ruin you. Don't you have anything good to play today?" Levine and I just looked at each other like Heckle and Jeckle, remember those two cartoon birds? We said, "No, this is all we have." I'm not going to say what we said about the man. But around a year after that I was asked to give a two-hour speech in front of two

Richard Oxman

L. Russell Brown at sixteen
with his first Silvertone guitar

hundred songwriters. I found out that they had asked one other person to sit on the dais with me. You guessed it—Al Steckler. Of course, Steckler never showed up. So, what I did was to speak to his empty chair for two hours. In short, I told the assembled if they ever listen to the Stecklers of this world rather than their own hearts, they would end up with exactly what was filling that chair beside me on the dais—nothing. Rejections still happen, and they're still painful, but when they do, I just think of my experience with Al Steckler.

Can you remember where you were the first time you heard one of your songs played on the radio?

I was in my car, and I got really excited hearing it for the first time. It was winter and there was ice on the street. When I tried to stop the car, it slid down the whole length of the block and rear-ended a car in front of me. I got out of the car with the radio

blaring, walked over to the poor guy whose car I just destroyed, and said, "I'm sorry. I was just listening to them play my song on the radio. I wrote that song!" The guy probably still hates that song today.

Was there any musical influence that you would have liked to have sat down and talked with?

The first would be Kurt Weill, who wrote *The Three Penny Opera*. I would have liked to have spent some time with him. And of course, Wolfgang Amadeus Mozart above all people. I'd like to meet Paul McCartney before I leave this earth. I think of him as the Mozart of our day. I love his work. But I did meet John [Lennon] at one time. I was doing a Billy Vera session at the Hit Factory and there were two studios with a little bench between them. I was sitting there on the bench, and this guy came busting out of the other studio and pushed himself down next to me. I look up and it's John Lennon squeezed up against me. Almost out of breath I say, "John Lennon, I'm Larry Brown. I wrote 'Tie a Yellow Ribbon' and I love you." So then John Lennon grabs me in a headlock and starts laughing and punching me saying, "That bloody, son-of-a-bitch song of yours. They just won't stop playing that bloody song. I can't stand it!" He's laughing and all the time punching me in the head. I said, "John, I probably copied it from you." And then he said, "Amateurs copy, professionals steal."

How would you describe yourself as a songwriter?

I'd only say one thing. I look at myself as a guy who never tried to write a song to educate anybody. All I've ever done was try to write songs to entertain people, give them a few brief moments of musical relief, something to remove them from the world for a moment and their everyday problems. Above all, I've just wanted to entertain.

What advice would you give to aspiring songwriters?

This is going to sound like the most tacky, pedestrian statement you're ever going to hear, but I'm going to say it anyway. Never, never, never, listen to anything but your own heart about what you believe in. Never give up on what you love. Never.

L. Russell Brown (on left) and Richard Oxman, both age seventeen

Wayne Carson on
"The Letter"

The Letter
Wayne Carson Thompson

Give me a ticket for an airplane
Ain't got time to take a fast train
Lonely days are gone; I'm a goin' home
My baby she wrote me a letter

I don't care how much money I gotta spend
Got to get back to my baby again
Lonely days are gone; I'm a goin' home
My baby she wrote me a letter.

Well she wrote me a letter
Said she couldn't live without me no more.
Listen mister can't you see I got to get back
To my baby once more.

Give me a ticket for an airplane
Ain't got time to take a fast train
Lonely days are gone; I'm a goin' home
My baby she wrote me a letter

Well she wrote me a letter
Said she couldn't live without me no more
Listen mister can't you see I got to get back
To my baby once more

Give me a ticket for an airplane
Ain't got time to take a fast train
Lonely days are gone; I'm a goin' home
My baby she wrote me a letter

Chapter 4

Wayne Carson

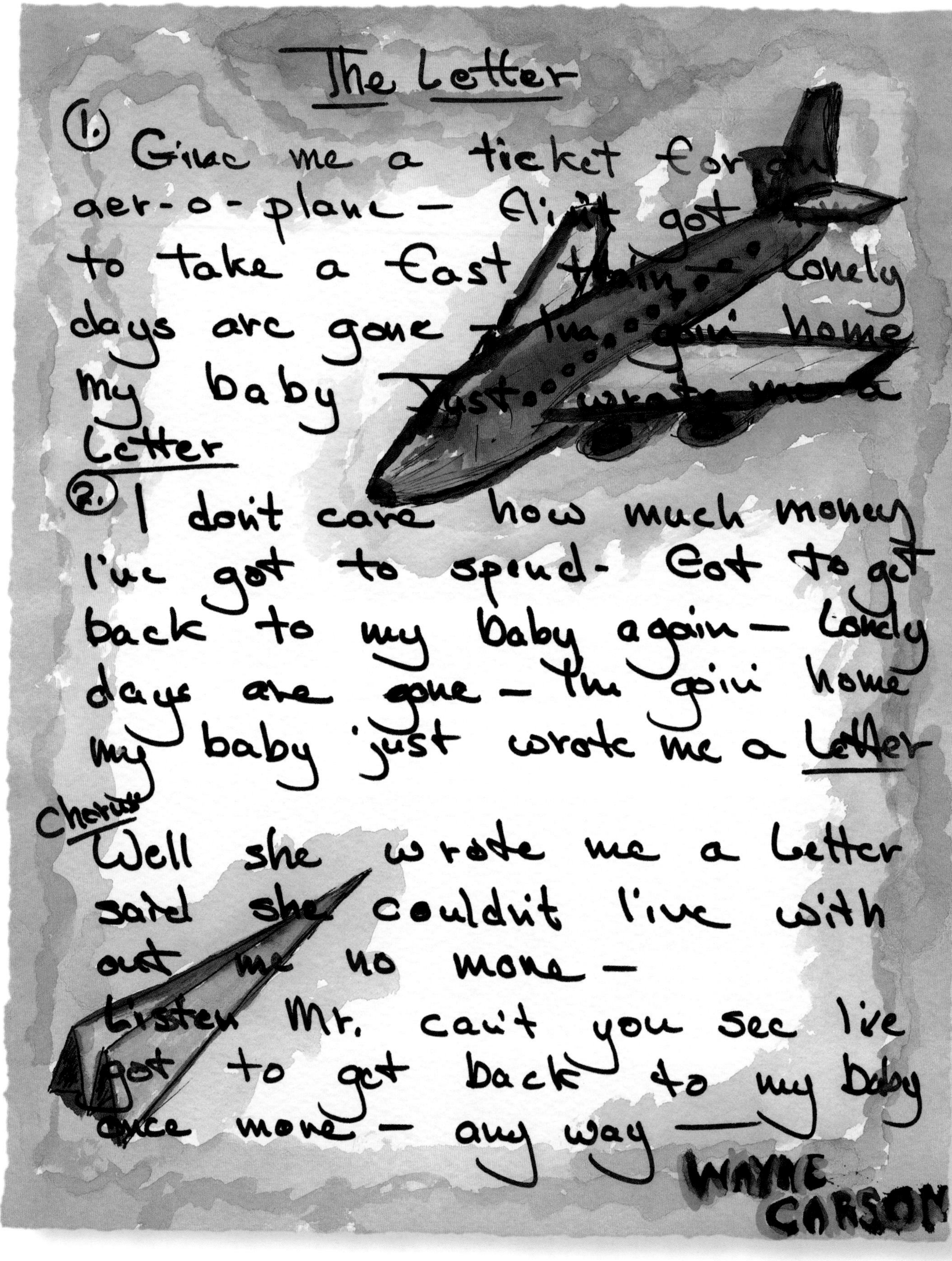

The Letter

① Give me a ticket for an aer-o-plane — Ain't got to take a fast train — Lonely days are gone — I'm goin' home my baby just wrote me a Letter

② I don't care how much money I've got to spend — Got to get back to my baby again — Lonely days are gone — I'm goin' home my baby just wrote me a Letter

Chorus

Well she wrote me a letter said she couldn't live without me no more — Listen Mr. can't you see I've got to get back to my baby once more — any way —

WAYNE CARSON

28

"One time when I was about fourteen years old, I came across a record my brother had bought called The Merle Travis Guitar. *I had a listen to that record and just said, 'That's what I got to do.'"*

"The other thing that started happening after I'd had a hit song was I'd be getting these phone calls calling me 'Mr.' Carson, but those were from the IRS. Suddenly, I had a partner in this business."

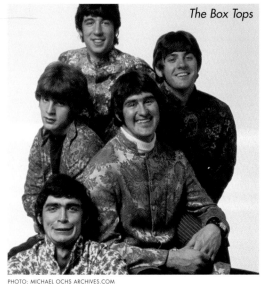

The Box Tops

PHOTO: MICHAEL OCHS ARCHIVES.COM

"The Letter," written by Wayne Carson Thompson, was recorded by the Box Tops for Mala Records in 1967. This was the group's first hit single and it held the #1 position on Billboard's Hot 100 for four weeks. Certified as a gold record, it received two Grammy nominations and has since exceeded BMI's four million broadcast performances level. In 1970, Joe Cocker released a cover of the song, which became one of the signature songs of his famous Mad Dogs and Englishmen tour. Wayne Carson was named to the Nashville Songwriters Hall of Fame in 1997 and currently resides in Nashville, Tennessee.

I was born in Denver, Colorado, in 1943. My dad had a big seventeen-piece western swing band called Shorty Thompson and His Saddle Rockin' Rhythm. When I was born, my family was deeply entrenched in radio, but that was the media back then. And after a while, I guess it turns into one of those subliminal things where you hear something over and over and then, suddenly, one day you wake up and say, "Boy, I love the way that guitar sounds." That's the way it was with me. I was surrounded by great musicians—people like Joe Venuti, the great accordionist Nick Perito, and all those great Dixieland jazz players and then, of course, my mom and my dad. My dad was the front man, more or less, but my mom was then, and still is today, a wonderful musician. She was a real prodigy. My Aunt Sally was as well, and they were both part of the organization. Having said that, you're around all that music as a kid but you don't think, "Oh, this is what I want to do." One time when I was about fourteen years old, I came across a record my brother had bought called *The Merle Travis Guitar*. I had a listen to that record and just said, "That's what I got to do." The people I work with say that if you have a natural ability as a player, you'll inherently always get to the right place. So, in my case, I have to attribute that to genetics and to my just being around music all the time, from the crib all the way through my growing-up years. So for me, I guess it was equal parts nature and nurture.

Has there ever been anyone you wanted to succeed for besides yourself?

For my parents, sure, but I guess it was also about a myriad of things for me. I just like the way the guitar sounded and I liked the way music felt. Of course, back then, it was a real time of change. Things were going from legit music, as we called it, to more of a pop style. I remember the sound of Mickey and Sylvia doing "Love Is Strange." Man, that just knocked me out. I thought, "How's he getting that guitar to do that?" I mean, Chuck Berry, Fats Domino, Little Richard, and James Brown, all of that stuff just knocked me over.

Would that include Elvis too?

Wayne Carson, 1967

Well, Elvis was kind of the icon for all of it. He really took what a lot of black people were doing and brought it to a mainstream, white audience with songs like "Hound Dog" and everything else he was doing. I grew up in legit music and, just like the musicians today, no one cared if you were black, white, green, Jewish, Indian, or Catholic. That never enters into the minds of musicians. Music does truly transcend all things. And I don't think, over the years, that all that much has really changed. The white guys are wanting to get a little more soul and the black guys are trying to get a bigger audience. Personally, I was influenced a great deal by Buddy Holly. Not so much Elvis, because I think that I understood right off the bat that by God, there wasn't ever gonna be but one of him. I think I knew that the first time I saw him, when I was thirteen years old, right up until the time when I finally met him. I played on an album that he did and sang some background vocals on "In the Ghetto." He was just magic, from one extreme to the other. On one hand, he was a simple guy from next door or down the street working at the gas station, but on the other he was absolutely, and I don't have any other word for it—electric. Not because of what he did, but because of the presence he had and who he really was in the flesh.

Did you think he was hard to get close to?

It was pretty tough to do. But one time, I was in the studio with him and a lightning bolt hit the damn transformer outside and knocked all the power out. So, there's all these guys like Marty Lacker and Red West just standing around. Elvis told them all to go get a sandwich or something and said, "I'm gonna hang at the studio with Wayne." So we spent the afternoon together in a candlelit studio, no electricity, just playing around with a wood bass, a piano, and a rhythm guitar. We were just shooting the shit, talking about a myriad of things. I think the one void in Elvis Presley's life was that he didn't have a friend, a buddy, to hang out with him who wasn't already working for him or who didn't want something from him. But that was the way Colonel Tom [Parker] liked it, because he didn't want Elvis to be just an average guy; he wanted him to be dependent and having to come to him for everything.

Did you get to hang out with him again?

Not exactly. That day, we talked about girls, we talked about motorcycles, talked about fishing. Fact is, he said, "I'll send the airplane after you." I lived in Springfield, Missouri, at that time and Elvis said, "I'll send my airplane up to Springfield and you load your motorcycle up and we'll take those fuckers down to my farm down in Mississippi and we'll hang out for a few days." Well, as soon as that got back to Colonel Tom, that never did come to pass.

Can you remember the first time you heard one of your songs being played on the radio?

I walked into the radio station where we had our offices in Springfield, Missouri, on the day a song called "Somebody Like Me," which I had written for Eddy Arnold, had gone to #1 on the easy listening and country charts. The girl at the reception desk, who had never paid me more than five seconds' attention in my entire life, suddenly got up, gave me a great big hug, and said, "Congratulations. I'm so happy for you." And I thought, uh-huh, this is different. This little gal had never cared about me or anything I was doing, and then all of a sudden, I'm favorable in her eyes. I wondered what the hell was so different about me from the day before yesterday when I didn't have a record on the charts.

Would you say being able to make a living as a songwriter changed your life in some ways?

That's right. The other thing that started happening after I'd had a hit song was I'd be getting these phone calls calling me "Mr." Carson, but those were from the IRS. Suddenly, I had a partner in this business. Not long after that, I was surrounded by accountants and attorneys saying, "Do you want to take this money and do this or do that?" At the same time I'm watching each one of them peel off a thousand here, and then another thousand there. And I'm saying to myself, "Jesus Christ, what's all this for? Where were they when I was starving to death over there in this little sixty-dollar-a-month house struggling to feed the kids?"

AIRPLANE ART BY WAYNE CARSON

What did you do with your first royalty check?

I went out and bought my family a house and made the down payment on it. My first house was a nice three-bedroom, two-bath, ranch house close to a golf course on the edge of town in Springfield, Missouri. It cost $17,200, and I think I put five grand down on it. That's what I did. I had a great partner in the business named Si Siman. He told me one of the wisest things anyone has ever said. He said, "Now that you have this money, and you can do anything you want with it, just remember this. You can get just as drunk on fifty dollars as you can on five hundred." And I never forgot that. So for the record, I took the fifty dollar route. He also said, "You're gonna find you have friends like you never even imagined before and they're gonna come at you from every angle." He was right about that, too.

Who are some of the people who influenced your music?

There've been several. One in particular was a guy named Joe Pass. Another was Grant Green, and I always wanted to meet Jimmy Wyble, Barney Kessel, and Keith Jarrett. Then there was also Charlie Hayden. Charlie and I grew up together in Springfield. His dad was Uncle Carl Hayden and he had a radio program for years on KWTO that came out of Springfield. He broadcast from right there in the kitchen of his house and he was one funny son of a bitch. The Hayden Family sang little old church songs, things like that. But Charlie was just about the best musician I ever heard. He gave me a whole different perspective and said, "Man, you are not a jazz player. You love it and dig it and I know you like what you hear, but it's not your thing, man. Your thing is a whole different bag. You're good at what you do; just stay with it and it'll happen." That was important to me. The reason I write songs is that I'm bored as hell with what's out there. Only occasionally do I listen to the radio. Most of the time, it's the same old repetitive thing I've heard and even done myself a thousand times. I don't say I've got better songs than most of what I'm hearing; hell, I know I do. When I first came to Nashville, the guys I hung out with were people like

Hank Cochran, Willie Nelson, Waylon Jennings, Wayne Walker, Roger Miller—people who really were writers. They had a big influence on me to be able to, by God, write a song and know that when you got done with it, it ought to stay written. Unfortunately, in this day and age, it's as much about the business deal as it is about anything else.

How do you feel about the state of the music business today?

I have mixed emotions about it. If my favorite music happens to be rock and roll, then I'm going to tell you "I don't hear any good rock and roll." These days I hear a lot of noise and a lot of meaningless stuff. I mean rock and roll is supposed to be "good time" music to begin with, and I'm not hearing that. I just don't hear any soul. Even in country music, I don't hear a lot of "meat on the bone." The proof of that is when some somebody does record a great song, it's really a smash. Take a song like [Mark Sanders and Tia Sillers's] "I Hope You Dance" for instance, now that's just a far superior song to anything else I've heard in a long, long time. I'd also go back to [Gary Baker and] Frank Myer's song "I Swear." That's a great song, an instant hit in both markets—country and pop, even R&B. But I don't hear those types of songs enough anymore. I turn on the radio and one song just seems to run into another. I think there are just too many damn amateurs trying to do it. Pandora's out of the box and she's done flew the coop. Anyone who can rhyme two words together thinks they're a songwriter these days. And that's the truth of it. There are plenty of great songs just sitting on everybody's shelves that never get recorded, believe me. Even in country music these days, they don't want to talk about drinking or cheating. But hell, the courtrooms are full, and there's a bar every eight feet, but nobody's "drinking"? And sure, there's a place for music that's just pure entertainment and I've been there, but there's even guys out there now who are running around onstage with socks on their Johnsons. I don't think people are having that much fun listening to music anymore. I've got people in my studio all the time, coming over here doing demos and sessions who can sing great. They have so much innate talent but they have to take a backseat to some other guy or girl who can't count to four in the proper sequence and wouldn't be given the time of day excepting they look so good. Nowadays, they got this little thing called Pro Tools [a computer program for music and sound design], and I mean you can take someone who's just awful and make them sound great up until the point when you hear them perform live, and then you say "Who the hell is that? Did the guy who made the record get sick or what?" Now it's all about a drum machine and some "ching-a-lings," but that's not R&B music to me. Percy Sledge was R&B, Joe Tex, the Isley Brothers, Martha and the Vandellas, that's R&B. So I guess to sum this all up, why don't you scratch everything I've said and to answer your question, you can just put down that music today is boring. It's just boring.

Wayne Carson was inducted into the Nashville Songwriters Hall of Fame in 1997.

Do you have any advice for aspiring young songwriters?

Well, nobody is ever going to teach anybody how to write a song. There are a few people around who will teach you how to "think" about writing songs. But it's such a personal thing; it's like your having faith. Nobody can teach you that faith. They can teach you about things that are in the Bible, but when it comes down to practicing it on a daily basis, you either got faith or you don't. The same goes with songwriting; you're either an original or you're a copy.

Steve Cropper on
"(Sittin' on) The Dock of the Bay"

(Sittin' on) The Dock of the Bay

Otis Redding and Steve Cropper

Sittin' in the morning sun,
I'll be sittin' when the evenin' come,
Watchin' the ships roll in,
Then I watch 'em roll away again.

Yeah! I'm sittin' on the dock of the bay,
Watchin' the tide roll away,
I'm just sittin' on the dock of the bay,
Wastin' time.

I left my home in Georgia,
Headed for the Frisco Bay.
'Cause I've had nothing to live for,
And looks like nothing's gonna come my way.

So, I'm just gonna sit on the dock of the bay,
Watchin' the tide roll away, ooh
I'm sittin' on the dock of the bay,
Wastin' time.

Looks like nothing's gonna change,
Everything still remains the same.
I can't do what ten people tell me to do,
So I guess I'll remain the same.

Sittin' here restin' my bones
And this loneliness won't leave me alone.
Two thousand miles I roamed
Just to make this dock my home.

Now, I'm sittin' on the dock of the bay,
Watchin' the tide roll away, ooh wee
I'm sittin' on the dock of the bay,
Wastin' time.

Chapter 5

Steve Cropper

PHOTO: ©EBET ROBERTS/
CHANSLEY ENTERTAINMENT ARCHIVES

"(Sittin' on)
The Dock of the Bay"

Sittin' on the Dock of the Bay
Watching the tide Roll away
Sittin' on the Dock of the Bay
Just wasting Time

Sittin' in the Morning Sun   I'll BE Sittin'
when the Evening comes
Watching the tide Roll in then I'll watch
it Roll away again.

CHORUS

I Left my home in georgia headed for the
Frisco Bay — I've got nothing to live for
Looks like nothing's gonna come my way

Chorus

Looks like nothing's gonna change
Everything still remains the same
I can't do what ten people tell
me to do so I guess I'll
Remain the same
Setting here Resting my bones
this loneliness won't leave me alone
two thousand miles die roamed just
to make this dock my home

Chorus !!!

Steve Vancross 99

"We moved to Memphis when I was about ten and that was the first time I heard real church music, black gospel music, and it blew me away. I remember thinking, 'What is that, man? That's incredible.'"

"Music to me has always been fun. My buddy Duck Dunn and I have a saying, 'We're not gonna make work outta this, are we?'"

Otis Redding

"(Sittin' on) The Dock of the Bay," written by Steve Cropper and Otis Redding, was recorded by Otis Redding for Volt Records just one week before Otis's death in 1967. It reached the #1 spot on Billboard's Hot 100 *and held that position for four consecutive weeks, earning a gold record. That same year, it won a Grammy Award for Best Rhythm and Blues Song and for Best R&B Vocal Performance. It ranks #6 on BMI's Top 100 Songs and has reached over seven million broadcast performances. In 1982, Waylon Jennings and Willie Nelson covered the song and received a Grammy nomination for Best Country Performance by a Duo or Group. Michael Bolton's version of the song reached #11 on the charts in 1988. Steve Cropper now lives in Nashville, Tennessee.*

I was born in my aunt's house in Willow Springs, Missouri, on October 21, 1941. My mom was there visiting so I was born in Willow Springs and not in Dora, Missouri, which is where I grew up and where my dad's from. Shortly thereafter, we moved to West Plains, Missouri, which is thirty miles from Dora. My earliest musical recollection is when I was a boy of maybe seven or eight years old, sitting in front of the radio and listening to *The Grand Ole Opry*. One day *The Opry* came to town. It had all the great original people, you know. I remember the Carter Family being on the show and I think June was probably about twelve years old then. We moved to Memphis when I was about ten and that was the first time I heard real church music, black gospel music, and it blew me away. I remember thinking, "What is that, man? That's incredible." Before that, I hadn't really heard anything except country music and a few pop things, like songs by Doris Day and Patti Page, things like that. Within four short years of moving to Memphis, I had bought my first guitar and was already writing songs. I had my first song, "Flea Circus," recorded when I was fifteen. It came out on the "B" side of a Bill Justis record called "Canadian Sunset." I got my first royalty check at sixteen, so I kind of knew what I wanted to do the rest of my life.

What does a sixteen-year-old spend his first royalty check on?

It wasn't that big of a royalty check. It was probably about thirty dollars or so, something like that. But not long after that I signed my first record contract, well, my first writer's contract with Sun Records, down at the famous old Sun Studios.

Do you have a special routine or a place you like to go to in order to write?

No, I've tried it all. I've tried it in a cabin and I've tried it on a boat. Truth is, most of the hits we wrote in the sixties were either written in the studio or in a hotel room. Because a lot of writers didn't live in Memphis, I'd wind up going to their hotel or motel room to write. And so a lot of the stuff with Otis [Redding], and definitely with Wilson Pickett, Don Covay, and Eddie Floyd, who I wrote tons of songs with, were written at the Lorraine Motel. That's also where Martin Luther King Jr. was assassinated. Sometime afterward, I went back to the place and stood on the balcony and said, "Wait a minute. The room right below us and the other one over there, that's where we wrote 'Knock on Wood.'" I forget what the room number was, but down the hall was where we wrote "Ninety-Nine and a Half." That part of the motel has since been turned into a museum.

Where do you find ideas for your songs?

I get ideas at all different times, driving in a car, brushing my teeth, whatever. I used to carry around a little tape recorder. Sometimes I'd follow up on what I'd put down, sometimes I wouldn't. But I usually work from a title. Almost every song that I've written, other than the instrumentals, the title always came first. Hell, the titles are the subject matter, unlike a lot of the songs in the seventies and eighties where the title has nothing to do with the song. I don't even know how people can remember the titles; it blows me away. They'll say "Baby I love you" four hundred times and the song will be called "Blue Marble." I've never understood that, but they get away with it and so they're cool.

Was there a person early on in your career whom you wanted to succeed for?

There were so many influences, but not really from a songwriting standpoint. As a young kid, I didn't live too far away from Elvis, so I had the pants like Elvis and the hairdo like Elvis. He was an influence, a look, and I got to be around him some, although not that much because I was too young. But some of our buddies who knew somebody got us into a lot of the skating parties, the movies, and the touch football games on Sundays. So I spent a lot of time at Graceland. Later on, we all got to be up at the house because our band, the Royal Spades, had a pretty hot reputation around town. Elvis knew who I was and we had a lot of mutual friends, but musically I was much more influenced by people like Lowman Pauling and the Five Royales, Chet Atkins, Chuck Berry, and definitely Little Richard. I was a big fan of Little Richard. Then all of a sudden Otis Redding came along and here's this guy that sings like the love child of Little Richard and Sam Cooke. I mean, he was just amazing.

When was the first time you felt like you were becoming successful?

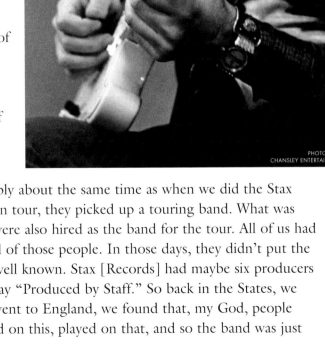

PHOTO: ©HENRY DILTZ/
CHANSLEY ENTERTAINMENT ARCHIVES

As far as having the feeling that, yeah, we achieved something, it was probably about the same time as when we did the Stax Tour of England in April and May of 1967. Usually when the artists went on tour, they picked up a touring band. What was unusual about this tour is that the guys who actually played on the record were also hired as the band for the tour. All of us had played on most of the records for Otis [Redding] and Sam and Dave and all of those people. In those days, they didn't put the musicians' names on the records, so we really had no idea that we were so well known. Stax [Records] had maybe six producers on staff and we all kind of worked as a team, so at best, the records might say "Produced by Staff." So back in the States, we didn't really get a lot of individual attention; only the artist did. When we went to England, we found that, my God, people actually knew who we were. They knew us individually, they knew we played on this, played on that, and so the band was just sort of walking around in shock. We couldn't believe it. In England we got treated like the Beatles, you know, and it was like "Wow." It was a totally different attitude when we got back home and then had to go back to work. Everybody felt like they were superstars for a brief while; it was really funny.

What was the first song you wrote that you heard played on the radio?

I guess the one I wrote when I was in high school for Bill Justis called "Flea Circus." It was a pretty catchy little ditty, but it didn't sell a lot of records.

Steve Cropper with his dog Easter at home in Los Angeles

PHOTO: ©HENRY DILTZ/CHANSLEY ENTERTAINMENT ARCHIVES

Did it help your love life in high school?

I've heard a lot of guys say you picked up electric guitars so you could meet chicks, why else? What is that Mark Knopfler line, "Money for nothin' and chicks for free"? Probably the first influential hit as far as my own career was concerned was a song called "Last Night." I played on the session, helped produce the song, and helped write it, even though my name wasn't on it. I held down a sustained organ note during the solo because Smoochie Smith didn't know the "book of matches" trick.

What's the "book of matches" trick?

You take a book of matches, just paper matches, and you wedge it between the two keys and the one note will keep playing. Booker [T.] used to do that and then he'd get up and walk away and the organ would still be playing and the crowd would go crazy. Of course, that got to be an old joke after awhile. "Last Night" did well enough to put us on *The Dick Clark Show*, but what I really wanted was to write and be in the studio. I love producing and playing sessions and that kind of thing so I left the band and came back for a while. After that we put together a rhythm section with Booker T. and the MG's. It wasn't too long after that we did "Green Onions" and by then we knew that we were capable of doing something great. We had quite a bit of success, but even though we had a big hit, we still didn't get to travel much and our pictures weren't even on the album. So there were a lot of cover bands saying that they were Booker T. and the MG'S.

Did you write more because you weren't touring?

Absolutely. We literally worked fifteen, sixteen hours a day in the studio. Now at this point in my life, that's all turned around and I'm doing just the opposite. I'm writing less and touring more and that's all due to the success of the Blues Brothers. Of course, for a long time after John [Belushi] died, we didn't do anything. Then we decided to pick it back up, toured Europe, and found out what a big fan base we had over there, so we've been touring over there now for fourteen years.

Was there ever anyone who tried to discourage you?

You know, early on in my career I was basically denied the opportunity to write. I guess it was a kind of reverse discrimination, because I was white and at an R&B label. Basically, I was accepted for my instrumental input; I just wasn't accepted for my lyric writing ability. I'd been writing songs since I was fourteen, fifteen years old and had pages and pages of lyrics for songs that had never been recorded. I had a couple of songs released, but Jim Stewart didn't take me seriously. Deanie Parker and I wrote a song called "No Time to Lose." So, rather than take it to Jim we went directly to Carla Thomas, Jim's favorite artist. She liked it, so Jim cut it. The song didn't do great, but it did well enough to get his attention and for him to say, "Hey, maybe Cropper can write songs." From that day to this one, I've been writing all the time.

Do you think in terms of music first or lyrics, or does that change from song to song?

I don't have any real formula. I've co-written almost everything I've ever done because I enjoy writing with the artists. Eddie Floyd and I were originally writing songs for Eddie to record, but then we had so much material that we wound up doing it on other people's sessions, you know, like with Wilson Pickett and Sam and Dave.

Do you think of songwriting as work?

I've never really looked at what I do as work. Music to me has always been fun. My buddy Duck Dunn and I have a saying, "We're not gonna make work outta this, are we?" Sure, when you get frustrated, writing can become work, but if it was supposed to be work, why would they call it "playing" music?

Have there been some songs that have been particularly tough to write?

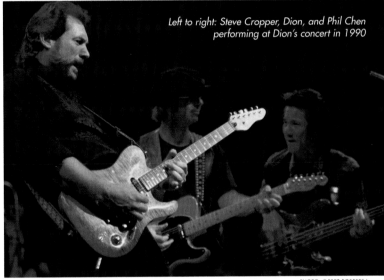

Left to right: Steve Cropper, Dion, and Phil Chen performing at Dion's concert in 1990

A lot of them have come easy and for a lot of them we had to stay up all night long. I guess I've written close to a thousand songs, but I don't remember a third of them. You remember the hits, the ones that did the best, because you get asked about them throughout your career. You're always reliving the night you wrote this, or the day you recorded that, or the day it first came out. But no one has ever asked me about the difficult ones before, and that's funny. I don't think it's ever really been difficult. There've been some songs that you can write in twenty minutes and then spend the next three hours trying to rhyme the last word in the last verse. "Dock of the Bay" came real easy because Otis had already started it. He had that intro and the melody and so basically, I just wrote about Otis. "Left my home in Georgia, headed for the Frisco Bay," all that was about Otis.

Is there anybody you've greatly admired that you never got a chance to sit down and talk to?

I usually get asked "Is there anyone you would have loved to have worked with that you didn't get to?" and every time I always say the same person—Tina Turner. I've gotten to work with so much great talent and I'm so grateful that I have had the chance to work with all these wonderful people. If I think about it, I'm just absolutely, totally flabbergasted.

Any advice you'd like to pass along to aspiring young songwriters?

At Stax, I was sort of the designated A&R [artists and repertoire] director. People were always bringing me stuff and saying, "Take a listen to this guy and a listen to that guy." We used to have Saturday morning dedicated to auditioning new talent. But before I let them leave the office I would say, "You know, this is really good, this is great, you're headed in a good direction here." I'd try to explain to them that it's great to be a performing artist and if you can achieve Elvis Presley's status, then more power to you. But the best that even Elvis could do was to have a single and an album both out at once. If you're a good songwriter, man, you can have fifteen or twenty songs out at once. If you can do that, then you're set up for life. Your best bet in this business is to be a really good songwriter and you'll outlast all of them. That's the kind of message I've always tried to get across.

Disc One
Track 7

David Crosby on
"Wooden Ships"

Wooden Ships
David Crosby, Stephen Stills, and Paul Kantner

If you are smiling at me
I will understand.
'Cause that is something
Everybody everywhere does in the same language.

I can see by your coat, my friend
You're from the other side.
There's just one thing I've got to know.
Can you tell me please, who won?

Say, can I have some of your purple berries?
Yes, I've been eating them for six or seven weeks now.
Haven't got sick once.
Prob'ly keep us both alive.

Wooden ships on the water, very free, and easy.
Easy, you know the way it's supposed to be.
Silver people on the shoreline let us be.
Talkin' 'bout very free and easy

Horror grips us as we watch you die.
All we can do is echo your anguished cries.
Stare as all human feelings die.
We are leaving, you don't need us.

Go take a sister then by the hand.
Lead her away from this foreign land.
Far away, where we might laugh again.
We are leaving, you don't need us.

And it's a fair wind
Blowin' warm out of the south, over my shoulder.
Guess I'll set a course and go.

Chapter 6

David Crosby

PHOTO: MICHAEL OCHS ARCHIVES.COM

David Crosby

Wooden Ships

David Crosby

If you smile at me
I will understand
'Cause that is something
Everybody everywhere does
In the same language

Wooden ships on the water
Very free and easy
Easy you know
the way its supposed to be
Silver people on the shoreline
let us be - very free - and easy
Go take a sister by the hand
lead her away from this foreign land
far away where we might laugh again
we are leaving - you don't need us
Horror grips us as we watch you die
all we can do is echo your anguished cries
Stare as all human feelings die
we are leaving - you don't need us
and its a fair wind blowin warm
Out of the south over my shoulder
Guess I'll set a course and go

"I've always wished I could have spent more time talking to Pete Seeger. . . . He's affected every singer-songwriter in this country in the last fifty years. Even if it's just as a secondary influence, he's affected someone else who's affected you. You couldn't possibly have gotten through musical life in this country without having been touched by him."

"To be here now, alive, playing music with my little six-year-old boy whom I might never have seen get born—hey, you know, it's pretty wonderful."

Crosby, Stills & Nash

"Wooden Ships," written by David Crosby, Stephen Stills, and Paul Kantner was recorded by Crosby, Stills & Nash for Atlantic Records in 1969. This song, a sentimental favorite of Crosby's, is on the self-titled Crosby, Stills & Nash *album, which was inducted into the Grammy Hall of Fame in 1999. As a founding member of the folk/rock group the Byrds, Crosby has also had #1 hits with recordings of "Mr. Tambourine Man" and "Turn! Turn! Turn!" Crosby, Stills & Nash was inducted into the Rock and Roll Hall of Fame in 1997, as was the Byrds in 1991. David Crosby lives in Los Angeles, California.*

I was born in Los Angeles, California, in 1941. I think the West Coast is a much looser place than the rest of the country. It was the last part of the country that was settled and therefore is the most rootless, which allows for more change. The longer a society is rooted in a particular place the more stultified it gets; the place with the least roots holding it in place is California, I think.

Would you say songwriting is 99 percent inspiration?

Ninety-nine percent inspiration sounds about right. I wish I could sit down and noodle around with the guitar or piano and just make it happen. And, of course, I do that just like other writers, but there's a part of my brain that becomes active at night just as I fall asleep and the other voice that I'm talking to you in right now gets dialed down. Sometimes I'll fall asleep and then sit bolt upright and grab a pad and pencil. Sometimes it's a melody looking for a lyric and sometimes a set of lyrics looking for a song. I admire writers who can get up in the morning, have a cup of coffee, sit down, and say, "I'm going to write a hit song now." Don't get me wrong, some can, but I can't. I wish I was in control of whatever it takes, but it's more like whatever you want to call it controls me.

What do you hear first, lyrics or melody?

It comes at me from all different directions. I have a set of lyrics bouncing around in my head right now and an entire melody, but they don't fit together. So, I'll just have to wait for the muse to help me out on this one.

What kind of music did you listen to growing up?

It was an unusual mix. I grew up listening to a lot of classical music and a lot of folk music. My mother always listened to music around our house. On the folk music side, she'd listen to the early Weavers, Odetta, Josh White, people like that. At some point my brother turned me on to fifties jazz, so I suppose I was also influenced by people like Gerry Mulligan, Chet Baker, Dave Brubeck, and musicians of that era. That, of course, led quite naturally to Miles [Davis] and "Trane" [John Coltrane]. There was very little pop music back then that interested me. I think the only artists who really got through to me were the Everly Brothers. The first time I heard them was on the radio doing "Wake Up Little Susie." The first song of theirs I learned to sing was "All I Have to Do Is Dream."

Was there anyone early on in your career that you wanted to succeed for other than yourself?

No, not really. I mean, I loved my parents, but this was sort of a natural thing for me to do. I started singing harmony when I was about six, or so they tell me. My brother showed me how to play guitar and I loved that. For a while there, in my teens, I even toyed with the idea of becoming an actor, but music pulled me way too hard. As soon as I started performing in coffeehouses, I pretty much knew that's what I wanted to do. The first place I played was in Santa Barbara, at the Noctambulist, which means "night walker" or "sleepwalker." In L.A., I played a club called the Unicorn and then the Troubadour came along and I played there. On Monday nights, there was open mike. But I wasn't even good enough to get hired. After that, I pretty much took off and went across the country as a folksinger. When I got to New York, that's when things started to get more serious, and for the first time I started to be able to hold my own and earn a meager living.

David Crosby and Graham Nash, 1970

When did you finally feel you had achieved some recognition?

I didn't have any popular recognition until the Byrds. The Byrds, you know, was a raving success right away.

What was it like going home after that?

Well, you know, people like to think that fame changes them—that they somehow get transcended into another "being" when they get famous. I don't think that's true. I just don't look at myself the way other people do. Man, somehow early on my compatriots and I saw that it was a trap and I've been lucky enough not to buy into that too much.

Are some songs harder to write than others?

The hardest was "Rusty and Blue." I can't really say why, other than the pieces of the puzzle just wouldn't come together. As for the easiest, there are many and no single one comes to mind. Maybe it's that they just seem easy because I was having so much fun doing what I do.

Was there anyone who was a musical influence on you whom you never got a chance to sit down with and talk to?

I've always wished I could have spent more time talking to Pete Seeger. I think he's a truly exemplary human being. He's affected every singer-songwriter in this country in the last fifty years. Even if it's just as a secondary influence, he's affected someone else who's affected you. You couldn't possibly have gotten through musical life in this country without having been touched by him. I also got a chance to hang out with the Beatles quite a bit; they were the other major, major influence on me. But I don't think there are too many people that I really wanted to talk to or get to know that I haven't actually had a chance to. In a long career you get to meet just about everybody.

It's no secret that for a while you were very ill. Did that experience change you?

I think it was a major eye opener. I can remember guys coming back from Vietnam who, if they weren't completely damaged by the experience, would have this kind of happy look on their faces like, "My God, I'm alive. This is fucking wonderful!" Many more of them were obviously drastically damaged by it, but the ones that didn't come home as damaged just came home extremely happy to be alive because no one was trying to kill them today. Well, I felt sort of like that. I felt then and still feel now so blessed for each and every minute of my day. I've always been a kind of happy guy and very much in love with life, but all that has increased seriously. I came very close. I was, like, maybe a week from being dead, they tell me. To be here now, alive, playing music with my little six-year-old boy who otherwise I never would have seen get born—hey, you know, it's pretty wonderful.

As a songwriter, do you have any specific strengths and weaknesses?

I'd have to say my strong point is melody and perhaps the interesting changes I can somehow weave into the fabric of the song. My weak point is simply that I write too many ballads and not enough rock and roll.

What do you think of the current state of songwriting?

I think the current state of songwriting is fine; there are plenty of young songwriters coming up who have immense talent. The current state of the music business is a fucking disaster, because it doesn't recognize

David Crosby,
Crosby, Stills & Nash Tour,
Los Angeles, 2000

that talent. The problem with the music business right now is that it's selling more of a theatrical experience than a musical experience. It's concerned almost entirely with surface rather than substance. So a good singer-songwriter doesn't stand a chance of breaking into the business or being able to sell records until that changes. The dark side of MTV is that it's turned music into a theatrical experience rather than a musical one.

So where does that leave the artist who relies only on his or her music?

Record companies see artists like us [Crosby, Stills & Nash] and James Taylor and Joni Mitchell and Jackson Browne and Randy Newman and other artist-songwriters as anachronisms, as dinosaurs left over from a previous ice age. I think they wish to hell we'd go away. Because what they really want to do is market cute little kids that they can hire by the pound and then dispose of when they're done with them. That's the nature of the business right now. I mean, a year ago, one quarter of the music business was run by a whiskey company [Seagrams], okay? Then they sold it to a French water company [Vivendi]. Now how much do you think they know about music? They don't. They know what a quarterly report is. Record companies, once they've been turned into conglomerates, have done as much to damage music as MTV and VH1 have by turning it into a theatrical experience rather than a musical one. The bigger a company gets, the less it cares about its product or the people it's trying to sell it to. It cares about its quarterly report, a better parking space, and knifing the next guy in line for a better job. That's the nature of the business. Music companies used to be run by guys like Ahmet Ertegun, Mo Ostin, Hale Milgrim, and Joe Smith, people who really loved music. Ahmet could go to a Ray Charles show and cry. These are the "real guys," the ones who started out as record collectors, the ones who loved music, who built our business. They operated on passion, not just numbers from a ledger. It's what is missing today.

Any particular artist or song out there at the moment that has your respect?

Accidents happen and a few get through. I mean, Shawn Colvin had a hit with "Sunny Came Home" [written by Shawn Colvin and John B. Leventhal], which was a brilliant record by certainly one of the best singers in the world, an absolutely great songwriter. But that was six years ago and it was an accident, an aberration. Where's the Springsteen record that should be on the air? Where's the James Taylor record on the air? We're talking about the best we got, man, where are their records?

Any regrets?

I have no real regrets. I think Stephen and Neil and Graham and I could have been a lot better at dealing with each other and made a lot more music. But you know, we didn't have an instruction booklet. None of us really knew what we were doing. And for all that, we did produce a bunch of really fine songs. We did it again last night and we'll continue to do it for some time to come, knock on wood. I think a person's art is a window into his soul. The art I've been making for the last few years, especially since I met my son James, has been very good, so my soul must be pretty happy with its lot in life.

Do you have any advice for aspiring songwriters?

The simple answer is don't do it for the money. Do it because you're compelled to do it, do it because you love it, do it because you have no other choice. With luck, the rest will follow, and if it doesn't, at least you'll know that following your heart is never the wrong idea.

David Crosby,
Crosby, Stills, Nash & Young Tour
Savis Center, St. Louis, 2002

*Sonny Curtis on
"I Fought the Law"*

I Fought the Law
Sonny Curtis

*Breakin' rocks in the hot sun
I fought the law and the law won
I fought the law and the law won*

*I miss my baby and the good fun
I fought the law and the law won
I fought the law and the law won*

*I left my baby and I feel so bad
I guess my race is run
She's the best girl that I ever had*

*I fought the law and the law won
I fought the law and the law won*

*Robbin' people with a zip gun
I fought the law and the law won
I fought the law and the law won*

*I needed money 'cause I had none
I fought the law and the law won
I fought the law and the law won*

*I left my baby and I feel so bad
I guess my race is run
She's the best girl that I ever had*

*I fought the law and the law won
I fought the law and the law won*

Chapter 7

Sonny Curtis

PHOTO: ROGER SEALY

"I started on the guitar. I was so young when I started, my fingers wouldn't reach across the neck so I could only play on the top four strings. Then one day, I remember I was able to reach across the neck and then I just started playing the whole thing."

"I was so dumb, I can't believe this. I went onstage just before Hank Snow came out and sang all of his songs, trying to impress him."

The Bobby Fuller Four

PHOTO: MICHAEL OCHS ARCHIVES.COM

"I Fought the Law," written by Sonny Curtis, originally for the Crickets, was recorded by the Bobby Fuller Four for Mustang Records in 1966. It climbed Billboard's Hot 100 *for eight weeks and peaked at #9. Among the artists who have covered the song are Hank Williams Jr., Roy Orbison, Bryan Adams, and the Clash. BMI awarded "I Fought the Law" a Citation of Achievement for reaching over three million broadcast performances. Sonny Curtis was inducted into the Nashville Songwriters Hall of Fame in 1991 and currently lives in Nashville, Tennessee.*

I was born on May 9, 1937, in Meadow, Texas. The main reason my brothers and my sister and I were interested in music was there was hardly anything else to do around there for entertainment. My aunts and uncles were all musically inclined and, in fact, one uncle played guitar and sang with Bill Monroe and His Bluegrass Boys. They were all a huge influence on me as role models and as [guitar] pickers. They were ranchers and lived a hundred miles away in Demit, Texas. We used to go up and see them; they'd bring out their instruments and play. I remember really enjoying that as a kid. Also around Meadow, we had musical Saturday nights. Everybody would bring their instruments and sit around an old piano and just sing the songs of the day. This was back before television, and of course, there was radio, but if you wanted to just hang out and visit with people, this was a good way to do it.

What comes first for you, music or lyrics?

It depends. I prefer to write by myself, actually. That way I not only can do it the way I want to, but I can take as long as I want. I usually just start staring at a blank piece of paper and take a melodic "hook" and see if I can't build something around it. Sometimes I'll just start singin' some words and not even have a hook. Of course, you ultimately have to arrive at a hook. If you co-write with somebody, then that's a different process. A lot of the time you have to throw out some titles and say, "Let's go at it from this direction." It seems to work differently just about every time. As a matter of fact, there's a lot of times when I'm finished that I'm amazed that I've actually written a song. It's hard to even remember the process exactly. It's like you sort of dreamed it, you know?

What was your first instrument?

I started on the guitar. I was so young when I started, my fingers wouldn't reach across the neck so I could only play on the top four strings. Then one day, I remember I was able to reach across the neck and then I just started playing the whole thing.

Were you more influenced by the music your family played than the music on the radio?

Yes. My two older brothers played and sang mostly bluegrass music. Eventually, I was listening to the radio a lot, so I heard Bill Monroe, Flatt and Scruggs, and all those early bluegrass bands. I even got to play on the radio when I was ten or eleven years old, something like that. The local station out of Lubbock had a big Saturday night jamboree affair, a kind of *Grand Ole Opry, Louisiana Hayride* deal. We'd go up there and play and it was then that I started to realize there was a big wide world of music out there.

Was there someone in your life you felt you wanted to prove yourself to or succeed for in terms of your music?

I don't know that I can remember ever wanting to prove myself to anyone. For a while, I wanted to be a professional baseball player. I can't recall when that changed exactly, but after that, all I ever wanted to be was a country singer and guitar picker. I had a lot of contemporaries around the neighborhood like Buddy Holly, Bob Montgomery, and Waylon Jennings; we all grew up together.

In 1949 Sonny Curtis entered the annual Harvest Festival's Old Time Fiddler's Contest in Brownfield, Texas. He didn't win that year, but a couple of years later he won first prize and a check for thirty-five dollars. Sonny's older brother, Pete, is playing guitar.

Glen D. Hardin, for instance, who I went to school with in Meadow, played with Elvis Presley, and then there was Emmylou Harris and John Denver. So I can say I had a lot of help.

Do you remember the first time you heard something that you had written on the radio?

Recording in Hollywood, 1964

I never really thought of myself as a songwriter, even though I even used to write songs riding on the tractor out on my dad's farm. I'd make up rhymes in my head and just write them out like that. I remember a local promoter named Babe Stone who was out there in Lubbock. He used to promote these shows where he'd book big-name country artists like Marty Robbins, Hank Snow, Ernest Tubbs, and those kind of people and then he'd fill the rest of it out with the local talent like Buddy Holly, me, and Bob Montgomery. I remember one time he booked Hank Snow and I was so dumb, I can't believe this; so naive and still in high school. I went onstage just before Hank Snow came out and sang all of his songs trying to impress him. Then some guy with Hank pulled me aside and explained the way of the world to me. He said, "Son, those are his songs and if you're gonna make it, you'll have to write your own songs or find somebody else that does." So I immediately started looking around in Lubbock for somebody to write songs for me. And, of course, I had no success. So I said, "Well, I guess I'm gonna have to do it myself." I wrote four songs and sent them to Nashville. One of those songs, "Sunday," started to cause quite a stir and I started to get phone calls from some of the lesser known artists all saying, "We're gonna do it." Finally, Webb Pierce, who at that time was a huge country artist, recorded it. That was my first real success as a songwriter.

Are there any artists you wish you had met?

I was always a big fan of Andrés Segovia, the classical guitar picker. He was always sort of an "untouchable" to me, and I never got a chance to meet him. I suppose he'd be the one. But I've been lucky that way. I've gotten to meet a lot of my heroes. I was a big Chet Atkins fan for a long time and, eventually, I got to meet him and we became friends.

What does it take to put you in the mood to write?

I have to be inspired; sometimes all it takes is a great piece of music. For instance, [Andrés] Segovia might inspire me or [Arthur] Rubinstein or Chet Atkins or the Beatles or songs by great writers like Simon and Garfunkel. When I hear a great song, it makes me think, "Oh man, I need to do something cool like that." But I've never been one of those writers that could go to work like a banker doing a job. There are some that can and I think that's terrific. I know one writer that gets up every morning, goes to work, writes, takes a coffee break and a lunch break, then goes home at night and forgets about it. He does the same thing day in and day out and then takes a two-week vacation. It's a job to him, and while I'm not saying that he doesn't write great songs, it's very different than what I do. Harlan Howard, who just passed away yesterday, was another one of those guys. But don't get me wrong. I have tremendous respect for these guys; they're absolutely magnificent songwriters. All I'm saying is I'm not quite that way even though I once worked like that myself. Before I moved to Nashville, I worked in Los Angeles writing jingles and it was an incredibly rewarding experience, mainly because of my old partner, Don Piestrup, who I thought was a musical genius. I learned so much by just hanging out with him and we wrote a lot together. The last four years I worked in L.A. with him, it got to be like a factory kind of a deal. We'd be in the studio by ten in the morning and the rhythm section would come in. Then at two, we'd do the horns, the strings, and the voiceover. When the engineer started mixing it all together, we'd go meet with tomorrow's client and then come back to the studio to write the next one.

What kind of jingles?

We did hamburgers, cars, and motorcycles. We did Buick, Chrysler, McDonald's, Burger Chef, Western Airlines, Continental, Knudsen, Honda, Suzuki, and Yamaha, just to name a few off the top of my head. We were really churning them out.

Is there anything in particular that can easily distract you from working?

I can get distracted pretty easily. One thing about songwriting, though, you can always put it in a drawer and then come back to it. This is one of the rules I learned from Harlan Howard. Sometimes if you just get hopelessly stuck, hopelessly adrift and you can't seem to get it, don't ever throw it away. Put it in a drawer, let it sit there for two, maybe three, months and then come back to it. All of a sudden your mind will be refreshed and you'll be thinking, "Why didn't I think of this back then?"

Did you have any formal musical training?

I grew up without any formal musical training; I'm what you would call self-educated. I wish I had been more diligent in learning about arranging music and composing, counterpoint and theory, all that stuff. I think that would have helped an awful lot. When I did knuckle down and seriously study harmony, it helped me tremendously. Even at my age now, I'm studying Brahms trombone parts and certain concerti, just to satisfy my curiosity. I think one of my strong points is that I'm diligent about practicing. I do like to get better at my craft, playing guitar, and working my finger technique. I'm still diligent about that.

What would you say to someone who was thinking of becoming a songwriter?

For aspiring songwriters, all I would say is work hard and don't give up. And just because somebody doesn't like your work, don't let it discourage you, because somebody else might. You should be thinking that maybe you know more than that other person who doesn't like your work. I'd recommend to anyone wanting to be a songwriter that you should get as good as you possibly can on your instrument. Learn all you can and never stop studying; that's the really important thing.

The Crickets,
the rock group Sonny Curtis has been
picking with since 1957. From left to right:
Glen D. Hardin, J. I. Allison, Sonny Curtis,
and Joe B. Maudlin.
This photo was taken in 1997 before a tour of
the U.S.A. and U.K. with Nanci Griffith.

Jimmie Davis on
"You Are My Sunshine"

You Are My Sunshine
Jimmie Davis and Charles Mitchell

The other night, dear, as I lay sleeping
I dreamed I held you in my arms
When I awoke, dear, I was mistaken
And I hung my head and cried.

You are my sunshine, my only sunshine
You make me happy when skies are gray
You'll never know, dear, how much I love you
Please don't take my sunshine away.

I'll always love you and make you happy
If you will only say the same.
But if you leave me to love another,
You'll regret it all someday.

You told me once, dear, you really loved me
And no one else could come between
But now you've left me and love another
You have shattered all my dreams.

Chapter 8

Jimmie Davis

PHOTO: MICHAEL OCHS ARCHIVES.COM

Jimmie Davis

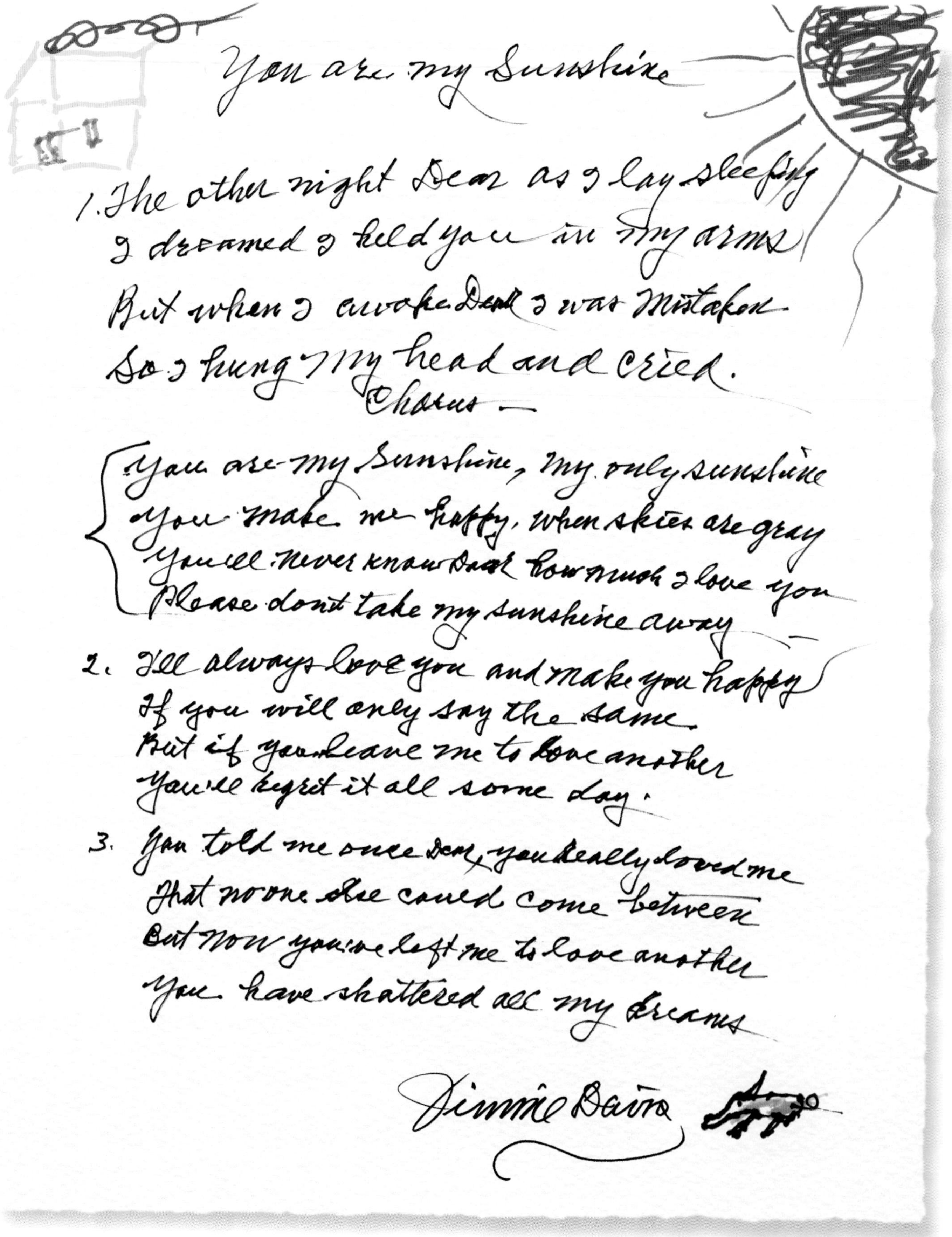

You are my Sunshine

1. The other night Dear as I lay sleeping
I dreamed I held you in my arms
But when I awoke Dear I was Mistaken.
So I hung my head and cried.
Chorus —

You are my Sunshine, My only sunshine
You make me happy, when skies are gray
You'll never know Dear how much I love you
Please don't take my sunshine away

2. I'll always love you and make you happy
If you will only say the same.
But if you leave me to love another
You'll regret it all some day.

3. You told me once dear, you really loved me
That no one else could come between
But now you've left me to love another
You have shattered all my dreams

Jimmie Davis

Jimmie Davis served as governor of Louisiana for two terms, 1944–1948 and 1960–1964.

"Later, even though he was very devoted to his obligations as governor and had much less time to spend on his music during his terms as the governor, he still considered himself to be a songwriter and performer who became governor, rather than the other way around."

Jerry F. Davis (nephew of Jimmie Davis)

"It's been a wonderful trip, and I've really enjoyed the ride. I just hope I've helped spread a little sunshine along the way." —Jimmie Davis

Ray Charles

PHOTO: CHARLYN ZLOTNIK/
MICHAEL OCHS ARCHIVES.COM

"You Are My Sunshine," written by Jimmie Davis and Charles Mitchell, was first recorded by Jimmie Davis for Decca Records in 1940. Jimmie Davis later served as governor of Louisiana for two terms from 1944 to 1948 and then from 1960 to 1964. "You Are My Sunshine" has since been translated into over thirty languages throughout the world and recorded by more than three hundred performers. One of the most memorable versions was Ray Charles's in 1962. "You Are My Sunshine," one of the most legendary and sentimental songs of our times, has become an integral part of the very fabric of American culture. Jimmie Davis, inducted into the Country Music Hall of Fame in 1972, was born on September 11, 1899, and passed away on November 5, 2000, at his home in Baton Rouge, Louisiana, at the age of 101.

The following are excerpts taken from an interview with Jerry F. Davis, Jimmie Davis's nephew.

One of the most memorable versions of "You Are My Sunshine" was the one recorded by Ray Charles. Did you ever speak with your uncle about what he thought of Ray Charles's version?

Ray Charles had recorded "You Are My Sunshine," "Worried Mind," and a couple other of Jimmie's very popular songs. They were wonderful recordings and Uncle Jimmie sincerely enjoyed them. Jimmie had a marvelous sense of humor which he usually delivered in a very deadpan and understated manner. Many of his jokes were in a self-deprecating style. He often referred to his own version of "You Are My Sunshine" as the "corn-fed" version, and to Ray Charles's recording as the "really good, wild version." His consistent comment about all of the different recordings that were made of his songs was, "I don't care how they sing them, just as long as they sing them." But he particularly enjoyed Ray Charles's renditions.

It was an extraordinarily well-covered song. Did your uncle keep a collection of the different recordings of "You Are My Sunshine"?

To my knowledge there is no complete collection of the recordings. I'm not certain but I think about five or six hundred versions have been recorded. Many of the artists sent Jimmie copies of their recordings. But those have never been collected or archived in one place.

YOU ARE MY SUNSHINE

WORDS & MUSIC BY
JIMMIE DAVIS
CHARLES MITCHELL

Featured by

JIMMIE DAVIS

PEER INTERNATIONAL
CORPORATION
1619 BROADWAY
NEW YORK, N.Y.

"YOU ARE MY SUNSHINE" MUSIC SHEEET:
COURTESY PEER INTERNATIONAL CORPORATION

Do you think it was difficult to get a song recorded in those days?

I realize that it is hard to get a song recorded and released today, but it may have been even harder in the 1930s and 1940s because the equipment and expertise to record and produce records was simply not as widely available as it is today. The recording industry was a much smaller club then and was far more tightly controlled than it is today. Until a performer "caught on" it was very hard to get the attention of the record labels. Jimmie had been working on "You Are My Sunshine" since the late 1920s and early 1930s, trying to get it right and trying to get it recorded. A gentleman named W. K. Henderson operated KWKH in Shreveport and Jimmie had a live show each week on that radio station. He mostly performed his own songs but he also sang songs by other writers. He was singing "Sunshine" in the early thirties and kept trying, although unsuccessfully, to get it recorded by a major record company.

He had his first really big nationwide hit with a song called "Nobody's Darlin' But Mine," but even that couldn't help him get "Sunshine" recorded. In the late 1930s, Charlie Mitchell, a player in Jimmie's band, started to work with him on polishing the song and to a degree, became a cowriter. Many years later, Jimmie bought back Charlie's share of the song. In 1940, Jimmie was in Chicago for a recording session of some of his other material and at the end of the session he persuaded the studio to let him record "Sunshine" and that was how it finally got recorded. It became an "instant" hit. Gene Autry and Jimmie Davis had been good friends for several years, and both Gene Autry and Bing Crosby went on to record the song. There were additional recordings by several of the big bands at the time like Tommy Dorsey and Guy Lombardo. Other big bands of the forties continued to record and play various versions of "Sunshine." It quickly became a widely known hit, as commonly heard then as any hit song today.

The question is often asked whether we know the identity of the lady the song was written about, or whether it was written about Jimmie's horse, Sunshine. The truth is that it was not written about a particular woman, or a child, or his horse. In the 1950s he bought a large beautiful palomino he named "Sunshine," and Jimmie and Sunshine made appearances throughout the country. One day in 1961, while he was governor for the second time, Jimmie rode Sunshine up the steps of the Louisiana State Capitol to have his picture taken. Then, on a whim, he rode Sunshine into the governor's office. When asked why he had done such a thing, Jimmie replied, "Well, Sunshine never had a chance to see my office." One of our state representatives said that that was the first time the "whole horse" had been in the Louisiana governor's office. Jimmie thought that was an enormously funny remark. But the answer to the question, "Which came first, the song or the horse?," is easy; the song was not written about the horse. The horse came along after the song had become internationally known.

When did your uncle stop performing and songwriting?

He was still writing songs, recording, and performing until a couple of years before he died in November of 2000. When he was in his early nineties, he was still giving at least one perform-

Shreveport, Louisiana, late 1920s

Jimmie Davis and His Gang
KWKH—1130 kc.

ance a week, but in his mid-nineties, he slowed down to about one each month. He would perform at gospel music festivals, country music festivals, and churches throughout the country. Many of his engagements were annual events which he returned to each year, like the one in Ithaca, New York. Whether he traveled to Minnesota, Kansas City, North Carolina, or somewhere else to perform, he always sang "You Are My Sunshine" and the crowd always joined in. I'm not sure, but I believe his last commercial concert was when he was ninety-eight years old.

Why do think he continued to perform at such an advanced age?

Jimmie simply loved to perform and interact with his audience. It brought him to life and it peeled the years away. You could see it take place. You'd chat with him five or ten minutes before it was time for him to go on, and by the time he got out on the stage, there was an entirely different person standing there. It was as if he was transformed by the sheer joy of being out there performing. It wasn't so much for the applause and adulation; he just loved to entertain people. After his performances, he'd sit at a table down in front of the stage where people would buy his cassettes, records, and books. He would autograph anything they would bring him to sign, whether it was a tape they had just purchased or their shirtsleeve. In his mid- and late nineties, he would sit there, sometimes for an hour and half, signing autographs and visiting with people. I'm confident that this was the key to his longevity.

Did they play "You Are My Sunshine" during his political campaign rallies?

Louisiana governor's campaign, 1943

PHOTO. BMI PHOTO ARCHIVES/ MICHAEL OCHS ARCHIVES.COM

Always. Without fail. The band was always with him on each and every campaign stop. He had a couple of rules about campaigning. Rule number one was to sing first, speak later, and then close with more singing. The second rule was to never say anything bad about your opposition, no matter what, even if it was true. If a reporter asked Jimmie about some scandal involving a political opponent, Jimmie would not take advantage of that opportunity to blast the opponent, but would answer by telling them something that he wanted reported about his own campaign, or by singing them a song. He refused to disparage any political opponent. He never responded to criticism from the press. When I was a young man he gave me a wonderful piece of advice, "Don't ever take on the newspaper unless you're prepared to buy it."

Was he surprised at his being blessed with such a long life?

As Jimmie moved into his late nineties, he had a distinct goal. He had been born on September 11, 1899, and was looking forward to New Year's Eve as the year 2000 approached. "If I can make it until then, the Lord will have let me live in three centuries." It's remarkable, but he did. More than once I've heard Uncle Jimmie say, "It's been a wonderful trip, and I've really enjoyed the ride. I just hope I've helped spread a little sunshine along the way."

The following are excerpts taken from an interview with Anna Davis, Jimmie Davis's second wife, who is now eighty-three years old.

Did Jimmie Davis like to be referred to as Jimmie or the governor?

I think he was secretly flattered to be called Governor, but when he was around music or in Nashville, he was always just Jimmie.

Jimmie cowrote one of the most beloved American songs of all time. Was he surprised at the long lived popularity of that song?

The song's popularity had happened quite a long time before we were even married, and we were married thirty-three years.

He wasn't a very emotional person and never expressed too much about how he felt about it. It was clear that he was very proud of the song and proud of what it had become, but he wasn't a man who was overwhelmed by much. I am quite the opposite and I am overwhelmed. But I can't really say just how he felt about the success of "You Are My Sunshine" because he simply accepted life so quietly.

When did you and Jimmie first meet?

I was in a group called the Chuck Wagon Gang. We were a gospel and country group from Fort Worth, Texas, and I started with them when I was a teenager. It wasn't long before we had heard about Jimmie Davis because he was in a neighboring state. Our group traveled in concert for, oh, years and years after the war and so did he. Occasionally, we'd meet up and have a backstage chat. He liked my husband, who was our guitar player, and both my husband and my dad respected Jimmie a great deal. But that's how we met, just through the concerts. His wife passed away, and about a year and a half later, my husband passed away as well. After that, it just happened that we appeared together, often on the same programs and that was how our life together started.

When he was governor of Louisiana, was music still a large part of his life?

Yes it was, and music was something he never, ever laid down. Of course, his first obligation was to his political life at the time, but he'd always manage to fit in a few performances, perhaps not as many and not as often as he would have liked, but no, he would never lay it down. He'd take the band with

Louisiana, late 1950s
PHOTO: BMI PHOTO ARCHIVES/
MICHAEL OCHS ARCHIVES.COM

him whenever he was politicking and always managed to get in a few numbers before he would speak. He knew how to get the vote of the people that way, I'm sure. Imagine the poor hapless political opponent who showed up to debate him after Jimmie had gotten the crowd behind him with a few "good ol' country numbers." He couldn't fail. He loved performing and he was always sure of himself. He went on the stage to entertain those people and he surely did. All my life, even coming from an entertainment family, I was always quite unsure of the audience, but he wasn't. He always knew what he should do and say for them, and he engaged the audience by talking to them between numbers. He was wonderful onstage.

Do you have any favorite songs of his?

Well, I like "Nobody's Darling." But then, "Sunshine" has to be high on my list because it's such a favorite with everybody. Children sing it all over the world and no matter what language it's sung in, Bantu or Russian, Portuguese or Polish, "Sunshine" has such a recognizable melody that you always know it. Do you know that song only has three chords?

What was your proudest musical moment with Jimmie?

That would have to be when he was inducted into the Country Music Hall of Fame about thirty years ago. I believe that was his biggest night. I was glad to be out in the audience alone so he couldn't see my reaction. He wouldn't have scolded me or anything like that if he saw me become emotional, but I always knew it didn't please him. And I must say, I always tried to please him, because he was quite a man.

Mac Davis on
"In the Ghetto"

In the Ghetto
Mac Davis

As the snow flies . . .
On a cold and gray Chicago mornin',
A poor little baby child is born
In the Ghetto.

And his mama cries . . .
'Cause if there's one thing that she don't need
It's another hungry mouth to feed
In the Ghetto.

People, don't you understand
The child needs a helping hand
Or he'll grow to be an angry young man some day.
Take a look at you and me, are we too blind to see?
Or do we simply turn our heads and look the other way?

Well, the world turns . . .
And a hungry little boy with a runny nose
Plays in the street as the cold wind blows
In the Ghetto.

And his hunger burns . . .
So he starts to roam the streets at night
And he learns how to steal
And he learns how to fight
In the Ghetto.

And then one night in desperation,
The young man breaks away
He buys a gun, steals a car,
Tries to run but he don't get far,
And his mama cries.

As a crowd gathers 'round an angry young man,
Face down in the street with a gun in his hand
In the Ghetto.

As her young man dies . . .
On a cold and gray Chicago mornin'
Another little baby child is born
In the Ghetto.

And his mama cries . . .

Mac Davis

IN THE GHETTO

AS THE SNOW FLIES.. ON A COLD AND GREY CHICAGO MORNIN' A POOR LITTLE BABY CHILD IS BORN IN THE GHETTO.... AND HIS MAMA CRIES.. 'CAUSE IF THERES ONE THING THAT SHE DON'T NEED, ITS ANOTHER LITTLE HUNGRY MOUTH TO FEED IN THE GHETTO.

YOU UNDERSTAND? THE CHILD HELPING HAND. OR HE'LL GROW YOUNG MAN SOMEDAY. TAKE A AND ME. ARE WE TOO BLIND TO SIMPLY TURN OUR HEADS AND WAY? WELL, THE WORLD TURNS.

PEOPLE DON'T NEEDS A TO BE AN ANGRY LOOK AT YOU SEE? OR DO WE LOOK THE OTHER AND A HUNGRY LITTLE BOY WITH A RUNNY NOSE PLAYS IN THE STREET AS THE COLD WIND BLOWS IN THE GHETTO. AND HIS HUNGER BURNS.. SO HE STARTS TO ROAM THE STREETS AT NIGHT AND HE LEARNS HOW TO STEAL AND HE LEARNS HOW TO FIGHT IN THE GHETTO.. AND THEN ONE NIGHT IN DESPERATION THE YOUNG MAN BREAKS AWAY - HE BUYS A GUN, STEALS A CAR, TRIES TO RUN, BUT HE DON'T GET FAR, AND HIS MAMA CRIES... AS A CROWD GATHERS 'ROUND AN ANGRY YOUNG MAN FACE DOWN IN THE STREET WITH A GUN IN HIS HAND IN THE GHETTO. AND AS HER YOUNG MAN DIES.. ON A COLD AND GREY CHICAGO MORNIN' ANOTHER LITTLE BABY CHILD IS BORN IN THE GHETTO.. ...AND HIS MAMA CRIES....

"It just seems that before I was of double-digit age I was whistling, making up my own melodies. I can remember my dad saying, 'What's that song you're whistling?' I'd say, 'I made it up.' And he'd say, 'I know you didn't.'"

PHOTO: GUY WEBSTER

"I'm such a perfectionist. I'm still rewriting 'In the Ghetto.' I still think I can make it better."

Elvis Presley

"In the Ghetto," written by Mac Davis, was recorded by Elvis Presley for RCA Records in 1969 and reached #1 on both the Cash Box 100 *and* Record World *charts. Elvis earned yet another gold record with this recording and received a Grammy nomination for Best Contemporary Song. "In the Ghetto" has had over two million broadcast performances certified by BMI. Mac Davis was inducted into the Nashville Songwriters Hall of Fame in 2000. He currently lives in Los Angeles, California.*

I was born and raised in Lubbock, Texas, the home of Buddy Holly, the Buddy Holly Freeway, the Buddy Holly Center, the Buddy Holly Walk of Fame, and me; I come from there, too. I was born in 1942 and left there as soon as I got out of high school in '58. I didn't much listen to the local music that was played on the radio in Lubbock, but being a rebel without a clue like a lot of kids are in their early teens, I found myself drawn to rhythm and blues. For blues music, I listened to these late-night blues radio programs out of Shreveport, Louisiana. I was in love with Little Walter, Little Willie John, Jimmy Reed, and all those people. I'm sure it worked its way into my music somewhat, but not very well because I didn't have the same kind of vocal apparatus they did. I always loved the blues, but in West Texas in those days, we basically didn't have any R&B stations. You had to search the dial for that stuff. Early on, I was influenced by Lefty Frizzell and people like that, and of course, Buddy Holly and Elvis Presley. When I heard Elvis for the first time I really, really went bananas. The next day I was all over town trying to find "That's All Right, Mama" but I didn't catch the singer's name. I thought they said Elmis or Elmand or something. Eventually I found "That's All Right, Mama" and listened to it in a little booth in the record store. Well, I couldn't afford to buy it, so my buddy and me just sat there and listened to it over and over and over again. We just about ran that forty-five all the way through to the other side before they threw us out of the store. Elvis was my hero at that time. In those days, I thought Buddy Holly was just a local guy trying to be like Elvis Presley. Suddenly, Buddy picked up and left Lubbock for a time, and then came back with this huge hit record. I remember sitting on my front porch and seeing Buddy driving by in a brand-new Pontiac Catalina convertible, the first year they made them. Now Buddy was not known for his good looks, but in that car with him were these two good-looking blondes. And I remember thinking, "Boy, this rock and roll is for me!" So my musical direction may have come from the Elvis Presley band, but my desire to get into the music business, you might say, came from those girls sitting in that car next to Buddy. I even wrote about it in a song "…if Buddy Holly could make it that far I figured I could, too." Clint Black later told me when he was seventeen years old he used to listen to that very song on my album *Texas In My Rear View Mirror* and used to say to himself "… if Mac Davis could make it that far, I figure I can, too."

Do you consider songwriting more a matter of hard work or inspiration?

One goes with the other. You can't write the song without the inspiration and you can't write a good song without a lot of hard work. I don't exactly know how to put it, but it's more like a fifty-fifty deal. Sometimes you can fall into a good song. I wrote "Watching Scotty Grow" in about forty-five minutes, but I was right there in my son's face when he was drawing his little pictures and the song came quickly. But mostly it's a fifty-fifty deal.

Do you have any special routine or place you go to get inspired to write?

Inspiration is like a bird that's going to land on your shoulder sometimes, but you've also got to catch it before it flies away or it seldom returns. I heard that somewhere. I didn't invent that saying, but that's the way it is. Once in a while I'll sit down with some guys and we'll try to write a song together. Other times I'll get inspired and a song will just come. Or I'll go out on the porch, get out of the noise, then come back in, and commit it to paper. I've written things in the car; I've written in my dreams. I don't have any particular set pattern, I guess. I can't just sit down and say to myself, "Well, today I'm gonna write a song." I'd end up writing a whole lot of bad songs.

When you're writing, do the words come first for you or is it the music?

It's more the lyrics for me. Melodies are, I don't want to say a dime a dozen, but they're all out there. For me, it's the words that don't come easy. In fact, I wrote a song once called "The Words Don't Come Easy" which said, "The melodies flow sweet and free when I bring my thoughts to you / The melodies pour out of me and they're fresh as morning dew / But the words don't come easy." You know, life doesn't rhyme, you have to work to make it rhyme.

When did you leave Lubbock, Texas?

I left there in December 1958. I got out of high school and moved to Atlanta, where my mother settled after she remarried, to seek my fame and fortune. That's where I got my start in the business. Fact is, I recently got inducted into the Georgia Music Hall of Fame, even though I grew up in Texas, because Atlanta is really where I got started.

Was the musical landscape in Georgia much different from that of Texas?

Atlanta suited my taste in music. R&B was very popular there but it wasn't what we call R&B today. It was mostly just the old three-chord turnover,

PHOTO COURTESY OF SHOWTIME MUSIC ARCHIVES (TORONTO)

blues and shuffle stuff, and it suited me to a tee. So, I put together this little garage band with a bunch of guys who hung around the swimming pool. We had a repertoire of about twenty songs and all of them were Jimmy Reed songs. They were all exactly alike except the lyrics were different. I could sound exactly like Jimmy Reed. I mean I really had him pegged. The music was all three-chord turnover: da do da, do da do, da do, like that. I had learned from Buddy Holly that you could go to a skating rink and people would skate for a while and dance afterward. So we talked this guy into opening the skating rink for us, at a place in Georgia called Misty Waters. The deal was we'd split every dollar they got at the gate as the kids came in to dance. They'd finish the skating sessions at ten o'clock so the kids could dance till twelve. We'd end up drawing like four hundred, five hundred people. And I remember when we were splitting up the money with this guy, seeing a good deal, he all of a sudden said, "You know, I got expenses here I didn't reckon on. I'm gonna have to pay people to keep my concession open and we're gonna have to set a limit here. You get your fifty percent of every dollar up to a hundred and fifty dollars, and the rest is mine." Sounded all right to us. We were just kids ourselves. Thing was, some Friday nights we ended up having fifteen hundred people come through the door. It was amazing. It was what it was, and hell, we were making good money, maybe thirty dollars apiece. You know the old Dire Straits lyric "Money for nothing and the chicks for free"? Well, that's exactly what it was. It wasn't long before we were the hot band around town and that lasted a few years. Then I got married and had a kid, so that kind of put an end to that. But I still wanted be around the business, I wanted to be near it. So I got a job as a record promotion man. Eventually I became a regional sales manager, traveled thirteen states, and worked out of Atlanta.

Mac Davis Show, 1975

What label was that for?

That was with a black label called Vee-Jay Records. They recorded all my heroes out of Chicago—Jimmy Reed, Jerry Butler, and the Blind Boys of Alabama.

Did you ever get to meet any of them?

Yeah, I met a lot of them. When they came to Atlanta I made sure I was there. My job was to hang out with independent distributors and the program directors at the local stations. In those days, it was mostly just one guy; not like today, where you have music directors, radio jocks, and program directors. The business has really changed now. I traveled thirteen states for years until Vee-Jay went down the tubes and went bankrupt. After a while I got offered a job at Liberty Records and I jumped at it. I worked for them in the same capacity for a couple of years setting up branches all around the country. In time I was asked to run the Atlanta branch or come up to L.A. and work in the publishing division. If I'd taken the Atlanta job, I'd probably still be there today in some shape or form. So I came to L.A. and started working with writers and record producers. I was trying to live in L.A. on the same salary I'd been getting in Atlanta, which was a big shock. Long story short, all this time I'd been recording songs into my little tape recorder. I'd send them in and they'd send them back, sort of like telling me to keep my day job. But all the time I was working at Liberty, I was meeting people, learning, finding out how to get things done and how to get records cut. That's kind of how I broke into the business. It's where I got my start.

When was the first time you felt you had achieved some real success?

For me, it was a hit song called "Memories," which I wrote for Elvis's comeback special in 1968. It just started flying up the charts because of all the TV exposure and also because it was a good song. This was after I had been working at Liberty for five years. I had put in lots of long hours sitting there writing till two, three in the morning; me, Delaney Bramlett, Larry Collins, and some other guys down in my little pigeonhole of an office on La Brea Avenue. Then all of a sudden, there I was driving down Franklin Avenue, and Elvis came on the radio singing a song I had written. I remember rolling down the window and turning it up, I mean real loud, and looking at the guy in the car who was stopped at the light next to me. I looked over to him and said, "I wrote this." He just looked at me like I was crazy. Man, was I proud.

A lot of people say there was a particular person that they wanted to succeed for. Was there anyone like that in your life?

For probably all the wrong reasons, my daddy. I didn't want to go into the business to please him; I wanted to do it in spite of him. It was like, "I'll show you that I can make money without having to do hard labor" like he'd done all his life. I don't think he ever believed there was a real job you could do sitting down. He didn't believe that writing music was a job, he couldn't grasp it—and to tell the truth, I didn't either at first. I honestly have no idea how I started writing songs. It just seems that before I was of double-digit age I was whistling, making up my own melodies. I can remember my dad saying, "What's that song you're whistling?" I'd say, "I made it up." And he'd say, "I know you didn't."

Was there ever someone whom you felt stood in your way?

No, I don't think that anyone ever stood in my way. As far as I remember, I was always encouraged. My daddy thought it was great when I started singing as long as it was in church. My mother, the rest of my family, everybody, absolutely encouraged me. I never had anybody tell me anything other than I was born to do this.

Did you have any doubts?

I think more than anything else it was hard to believe in myself. I always felt that I didn't deserve what I was getting. To me, even though I had what people might call a certain level of success, I felt I was so less deserving than so many other artists. I always felt like "Why am I here? This other guy's smarter than I am, better looking than I am, more talented." And I think it hurt me in a lot of ways. That's why, to be honest, I'd have to say if anybody got in my way, it was me. Hell, I'm such a perfectionist. I'm still rewriting "In the Ghetto." I still think I can make it better.

Was there anyone in particular who influenced your music whom you would have liked to talk to but never did?

You know, there's a lot of guys I would have loved to have talked to. But I did get to sit down and talk to Elvis a few times. Once when the Memphis Mafia left us alone, I actually got to talk to him, you know, man to man. This one night, after I had gotten to work with Elvis and knew him a little better, I told him how I thought he was losing it because everything was being filtered through these guys he had around him. After I'd had my say, Elvis said, "So what can I do to make this right?" And I answered, "Well, give me your home phone number." He called Charlie Hodge over and said, "What's my home number?" Charlie replied, "You mean the phone you answer at home?" Elvis said, "Yeah, the one I answer when you guys call me." Charlie

shoots back, "You sure you want to do this?" Elvis just said, "Just tell me what my damn home phone number is." When Elvis finally got the phone number, he wrote it down on a matchbook cover, handed it to me, and said, "Does that make things all right?" "Well," I answered, "I'll probably never call you. But you just went way up in my eyes." I just stuck that matchbook in my pocket and said good-bye. That was the last time I ever saw Elvis.

Where's that matchbook cover now?

I threw it away after I wrote the number down in my phone book. I kept the number in my book for probably fifteen years after he died. Strange.

Any advice you'd give to aspiring young songwriters?

The advice I've always given to songwriters is get yourself a really good day job. Something you like to do, something you're good at, and let that be your career. Write songs and create music as a labor of love. Work hard, be persistent, get lucky, and try and get your songs cut. Hone your craft, but always have something to fall back on because there's nothing worse than a bitter, starving artist walking around saying, "The world never gave me a chance."

Ervin Drake on
"It Was A Very Good Year"

It Was A Very Good Year
Ervin Drake

When I was seventeen,
It Was A Very Good Year,
It Was A Very Good Year
For small town girls and soft summer nights.
We'd hide from the lights on the village green
When I was seventeen!

When I was twenty-one,
It Was A Very Good Year,
It Was A Very Good Year
For city girls who lived up the stair,
With perfumed hair that came undone.
When I was twenty-one!

When I was thirty-five,
It Was A Very Good Year,
It Was A Very Good Year
For blue-blooded girls of independent means,
We'd ride in limousines their chauffeurs would drive
When I was thirty-five!

But now the days are short,
I'm in the autumn of the year:
And now I think of my life as vintage wine
From fine old kegs,
From the brim to the dregs it poured sweet and clear,
It Was A Very Good Year!

Chapter 10

Ervin Drake

PHOTO: DAVID WORKMAN

"It Was A Very Good Year"

17
When I was seventeen,
It was a very good year;
It was a very good year
For small town girls
And soft summer nights;
We'd hide from the lights
On the village green
When I was seventeen.

21
When I was twenty-one,
It was a very good year;
It was a very good year
For city girls
Who lived up the stair;
With perfumed hair
That came undone
When I was
        twenty-one.

35
When I was thirty-five,
It was a very good year;
It was a very good year
For blue-blooded girls,
Of independent means.
We'd ride in limousines.
Their chauffeurs
        would drive
When I was
        thirty-five.

BUT
Now the days are short.
I'm in the autumn of the year;
And now I think of my life
As vintage wine
From fine old kegs;
From the brim to the dregs
It poured sweet and clear,
It was a very good year!

by
Ervin Drake

"I wrote the whole damn thing out on a lead sheet . . . and went in and showed it to Arthur. He said, 'Don't bother to show it to me because I'm a song publisher and what the hell do I know about songs?'"

"There's no waiting for the mood. I don't call on the muse or any of that; that's all nonsense. There's nothing else. Sammy Cahn never waited for a muse."

Frank Sinatra

PHOTO: CHARLYN ZLOTNIK/MICHAEL OCHS ARCHIVES.COM

"It Was a Very Good Year," written by Ervin Drake originally for the Kingston Trio, was recorded by Frank Sinatra for his own label, Reprise Records, in 1965. Sinatra's recording climbed to #28 on Billboard's Hot 100 and received four Grammy nominations. It won two Grammy Awards: the first for Best Vocal Performance, Male and the second for Best Arrangement Accompanying a Vocalist. Ervin Drake is a past president of the Songwriters Guild of America and was inducted into the Songwriters Hall of Fame in 1983. He currently lives in Great Neck, New York.

I was born on April 3, 1919, in New York City into a house full of music. I had two strong influences—one was my mother, who was a very good lyric soprano and did a lot of singing around the house. The other was my older brother, Milton, who is seven years older than I am and retired now. He'll be ninety in August. He was a songwriter long before I was. He wrote things like "Mairzy Doats," "Java Jive," and "Nina Never Knew." Those are all his songs.

Is there anything special you do to put yourself in the frame of mind to write?

If somebody gives me an assignment, my pants bottom immediately hits the piano seat and I start. There's no waiting for the mood. I don't call on the muse or any of that; that's all nonsense. There's nothing else. Sammy Cahn never waited for a muse.

Is it difficult to be creative on demand?

Maybe this will be helpful to explain. One night I was walking through the halls of the 1650 Broadway Building in New York; I had seen some publisher or other and was on my way home. I walked past an open door and saw a friend of mine, Arthur Mogul, and he said, "Ervin, come in. You don't happen to have a song for the Kingston Trio, do you? You know, the folk group?" I said, "Not on me." Then he said, "Nick Reynolds and Dave Guard want Bobby Shane to do a solo performance on the next album, which is going to be called *Going Places*. I'd like to have a song for him and I don't have anything on hand." Mogul was the head of Reedlands, the Kingston Trio's music publishing company at the time. So I asked Arthur how much time I had to come up with something and was told that Bobby Shane would be in the next morning. "Terrific," I said. "You couldn't have called me, given me just a little more notice?" So I went to the piano room, sat down at the bench, and pulled out my diary. I can't remember anything so my life is run by what I put down in those annual diaries. I reached in there and found the place where I had notated ideas for songs and frantically looked through it. In just a few short hours, Bobby Shane was coming in, and I wanted to have something for him. I call that "target shooting." In other words, if a target presents itself, I want to hit that target. All of a sudden I read a note I had written that said, "Story of a guy's life told in wine vintage terms, possible title—'It Was a Very Good Year' (neo folk)." I mean, the whole thing was already written out there, and so I was off and running. I finished it in about a half hour. I deliberately wrote it as a modal piece to give it the "folk sound." You never would have known it from Sinatra's recording, because he slowed the whole thing down. Anyway, when I finished I thought, "This is going to be a very boring song unless I can stick in a 'separator,' something to come in with, separate out the verses, and then go out with." So I put in [sings], "Yum dada dum, yum dada dada dum, yum dada dum, bum bum / When I was very young," like that. Then I thought, "Maybe I ought to put in a few syllables of Elizabethan nonsense rhyme." So I put in, "Hi lurel li, hi lurel lurel li, hi dury dune dune dune." When you're stuck, you will settle for anything that comes along. Then I wrote the whole damn thing out on a lead sheet because I knew I'd never remember the melody, such as it was. I was through in an hour and went in and showed it to Arthur. He said, "Don't bother to show it to me because I'm a song publisher and what the hell do I know about songs?" Let's just say that Arthur is a very honest, very candid man. "Show it to Bobby," he said. "If he likes it, he'll do it and that's that." So I did and the rest is history.

When I was twenty-one, it was a very good year; it was a very good year for city girls who lived up the stair, with perfumed hair that came undone when I was twenty-one.

Ervin Drake, age twenty-one, with Edith, "the girl who lived up the stair" at their "village green" in Central Park, New York City, 1940

To this day, Arthur Mogul will call me up, let's say from someplace like Tanganyika in Africa and say, "I have some people here who don't believe you wrote 'It Was a Very Good Year' in twenty minutes in my office." "Arthur," I always say, "It took me a half hour to write it and another half hour to write out the lead sheet, so don't exaggerate!" But that's how the song was written. Years later, Sinatra made a marvelous recording of it and Gordon Jenkins orchestrated that passage starting with an oboe which added such a wonderful, mournful quality and presaged what was to follow. Frank Sinatra and I were sitting at Caesars Palace late one night and I said to him, "You know, you never saw fit to use those 'separation' words I wrote for the song." And he asked, "What separation words?" "Those Elizabethan nonsense syllables," I said. Frank looked at me and said, "Buddy, you're one lucky songwriter. If I had sung them they would've come out, 'Hey shoo bee do, hey shoo bee do bee do bee.'" I never get tired of telling that story.

Has there ever been anyone whom you wanted to succeed for other than yourself?

When I met my first wife, I kind of showed off for her. I remember taking her into the piano room and playing her some songs I had written. Showy kind of stuff that was never published, but which showed some of my particular talents. While I knew her, I had my first hit with the Portuguese tune "Tiko Tiko." Then I had a hit with a thing I had written the words and music for called, "The Rickety Rickshaw Man," which sold over a million recordings for Eddy Howard. Actually, I love to write songs. I've been writing songs since I was about twelve years old.

Can you recall the first time you heard one of your songs on the radio?

Around 1942, I heard a song on the radio I had written called "Do Something," which was recorded by the Horace Heidt Orchestra, and it was very exciting. Getting songs recorded was a different issue. I can remember when Art Thorsen, the manager for the Horace Heidt Orchestra, called me up because they wanted to record "Do Something," and they also wanted to be "cut in." There have been a lot of "cut ins" along the way. One of my most important copyrights, "Good Morning Heartache," was recorded by Billie Holiday, but before we could get to Billie Holiday, we had to cut in a young man named Danny Fisher. Years later, Danny Fisher referred to it as the greatest song he had ever written. It was the only song he ever "wrote" that he had nothing whatsoever to do with the writing. I finally told him, "Danny, if you don't stop telling everybody you wrote the lyric for this song, I will tell people the truth and it will embarrass you. So forget about it and be happy with what you've got." I think he stopped after that.

Budd Schulberg, author of the novel What Makes Sammy Run?

Actor Robert Alda

Actress Sally Ann Howes

1963 rehearsal of the Broadway musical What Makes Sammy Run? for which Ervin Drake wrote the music and lyrics

Ervin Drake

PHOTO: SAM SIEGEL

Were you at the recording session when Billie Holiday recorded "Good Morning Heartache"?

I was, and so was Irene Higginbotham [cowriter of "Good Morning Heartache"], a tall, slender, black woman who was a wonderful composer. She had this one song as her only truly popular hit. Anyway, she and I were sitting within three feet of Billie at the recording session and absolutely transfixed as they recorded Sy Oliver's arrangement, which by the way, was the first time anyone had ever used strings in recording Billie. I remember the sight of the "black spaghetti," those thin dark strips of vinyl coming off the master as the stylus cut into it. It was the first time I had ever seen that, and I thought, "My God, if anything screws up they are going to have to start this all over again." But everything was live in those days and of the moment. It's amazing how much good recording was done for all those years under those circumstances.

Was Billie Holiday as popular then as she is now?

No, definitely not. "Good Morning Heartache" was an underground hit for many years and was recorded many, many times prior to Diana Ross recording it for the film *Lady Sings the Blues*. It was really Diana Ross who had the first charted hit with it, she is really the one who put it on the map. But when it came to Billie, Irene and I were much too shy and just so overwhelmed by her presence. We didn't even go over to her and say, "Hello Billie, we wrote this song."

Was there ever anyone whose talent really inspired you and whom you wished you had met?

Oh, yes, Fred Astaire. I never worked with him and I regret that because I think he was a superb performer, dancer, actor, man—the whole thing. I got to meet Gene Kelly and I also got to know Frank Sinatra very well. Frank was such a generous and kind guy. He used to call me several times a year just to say, "Hi, Ervin, how you doin'? You need anything, you just give me a ring, okay?" He was the only performer I dealt with who ever did anything like that. He was a whole other kind of guy. From my point of view, there was nothing outrageous about the man except his generosity.

What is your favorite distraction?

My wife.

Are there any famous songs you wish you had written?

I wish I'd had the training to have written Gershwin's "Rhapsody in Blue" or "Concerto in F" or "Porgy and Bess"; yes, that I do wish. There is no point in thinking about it though, it's fruitless. It takes years of training and God, could Gershwin play those things. I have recordings of him playing and they are monumental. You know, when the Gershwins wrote "Fascinating Rhythm," they supposedly had this uncle who had reportedly said, "Boys, I love this song you're playing, this 'Fashion On the River.'"

Do you have any thoughts you'd like to leave for aspiring young songwriters?

A couple of things. Number one, I would tell them that if they are interested in writing, then from my point of view, I would say don't listen to most of the music that is out there today. If you are going to listen to "hip-hop" and "rap," you are deluding yourself because there is no music in it. There is just no point in keeping the gloves on about that sort of thing. I would say go back to the twenties, thirties, and forties, listen to Richard Rodgers, to Cole Porter,

BUT
NOW THE DAYS ARE SHORT,
NOW I'M N THE AUTUMN OF THE YEAR;
AND NOW I THINK OF MY LIFE
AS VINTAGE WINE
FROM FINE OLD KEGS;
FROM THE BRIM TO THE DREGS
IT POURED SWEET AND CLEAR,
IT WAS A VERY GOOD YEAR!

Howard Arlen, and Irving Berlin. These people are some of the foundation blocks of classic songwriting. Listen to what you can derive from them. And when it comes to lyrics, don't settle for non-rhymes. "Mine" and "times" never rhyme; they are assonance. "Light" and "like" are not rhymes; they are assonance. My advice to the aspiring young songwriter is don't make an assonance of yourself.

Ervin Drake,
age fifty-six

Disc One
Track 12

John Claude Gummoe on
"Rhythm of the Rain"

Rhythm of the Rain
John Gummoe

Listen to the rhythm of the falling rain,
Telling me just what a fool I've been.
I wish that it would go and let me cry in vain
And let me be alone again.

The only girl I care about has gone away
Looking for a brand new start.
But little does she know that when she left that day
Along with her she took my heart.

Rain please tell me now does that seem fair,
For her to steal my heart away when she don't care.
I can't love another when my heart's somewhere far away.

The only girl I care about has gone away
Looking for a brand new start.
But little does she know that when she left that day
Along with her she took my heart.

Rain, won't you tell her that I love her so.
Please ask the sun to set her heart aglow.
Rain in her heart and let the love we knew start to grow.

Listen to the rhythm of the falling rain,
Telling me just what a fool I've been.
I wish that it would go and let me cry in vain
And let me be alone again.

Chapter 11

John Claude Gummoe

PHOTO: VICTOR AVILA

John C. Gummoe

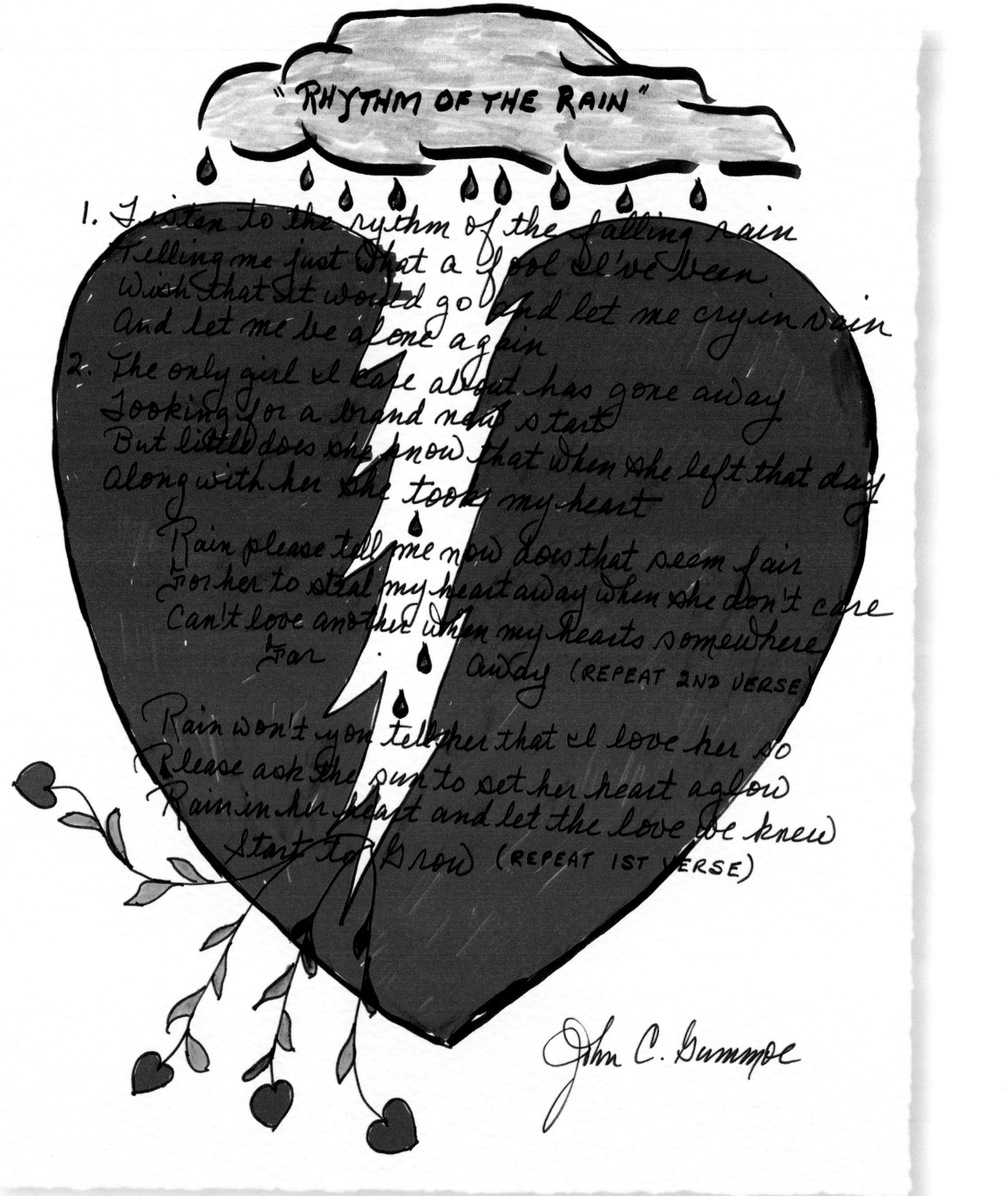

"RHYTHM OF THE RAIN"

1. Listen to the rhythm of the falling rain
Telling me just what a fool I've been
Wish that it would go and let me cry in vain
And let me be alone again

2. The only girl I care about has gone away
Looking for a brand new start
But little does she know that when she left that day
Along with her she took my heart

Rain please tell me now does that seem fair
For her to steal my heart away when she don't care
Can't love another when my heart's somewhere
Far   Away (REPEAT 2ND VERSE)

Rain won't you tell her that I love her so
Please ask the sun to set her heart aglow
Rain in her heart and let the love we knew
Start to Grow (REPEAT 1ST VERSE)

John C. Gummoe

84

"My grandmother . . . wrote hymns. . . . My father
wrote poetry as did my sister Jean . . . there's always
been that writing thing going on all around me.
So I suppose part of my desire to write was genetic,
and part of it was a need to express my feelings. . . ."

"Maybe it's a small thing, but I'd like people to know we were one 'kick-ass' rock group."

The Cascades

"Rhythm of the Rain," written by John Claude Gummoe, was recorded by the Cascades for Valiant Records in 1963. Rising on the charts for thirteen weeks and peaking at #3 on Billboard's Hot 100, *it has been covered by such diverse performers as Dan Fogelberg, Lawrence Welk, Percy Faith, Johnny Rivers, and Floyd Cramer, among many others. Ranked on the BMI Top 100 Songs list as the ninth most performed song, "Rhythm of the Rain" has received BMI's Special Citation of Achievement in recognition of over six and a half million broadcast performances. John Claude Gummoe currently lives in Los Angeles, California.*

I was born in Cleveland, Ohio, on August 2, 1938, into a dysfunctional family with an alcoholic father and a mother who had to go to work to support the family. I was pretty much driven by my circumstances. At some point, I decided that I didn't want to be my father's son and didn't want to go where he went with his life. I wanted something better. Even though I wasn't sure how I was going to do it, I decided I was going to do something great in my life, something worthwhile. So that's probably the only thing I'd say about being born and raised in Cleveland that ever affected my writing. Actually getting into writing and being a musician and a singer didn't happen for me until after I left Ohio and came to California.

Do you consider songwriting a matter of hard work or inspiration?

I suppose the short answer is it all starts with inspiration and that can be, and always has been, completely unpredictable. An idea for a song, or even a melody for that matter, can come from almost anywhere. Once inspiration has struck, then it's a matter of working and fashioning it into a song, and every song is different.

Was there much music in your family?

Quite a lot. My sister Dorothy sang on the radio when she was a child. We used to stand around the kitchen sink and sing harmony together. I found I was gifted with a natural ear for chords and an ear for harmony, so we did a lot of that. I'm also distantly related to Brewster Higley, who wrote "Home on the Range." My grandmother also wrote hymns. When I say she wrote hymns, I mean she just wrote the lyrics to hymns, not the music. My father wrote poetry as did my sister Jean, who's had a few things published in women's magazines. But there's always been that writing thing going on all around me. So I suppose part of my desire to write was genetic, and part of it was a need to express my feelings—take the things that you normally wouldn't talk about and put them into a song.

What did your dad do for a living?

My dad was a security cop at Cleveland Graphite Bronze. Because he was an alcoholic, he was often fired when he was working. But he was also a frustrated writer. We're talking around the time of the Second World War when things were pretty tough for everybody. So my early beginnings were meager, as were those of many people at that time, and I was mostly raised by a single parent. My mother and dad split up when I was five. At that point I went to live with my oldest sister. If you can picture this, I was five years old and my sister was newly married at eighteen. She took me under her wing because my mother was working and so there wasn't anybody else to really look after me. She raised me in her home until I was about thirteen, and then I went back to live with my mother.

Did you always want to be in the music business?

I had no idea that I would ever end up in the music business, let alone have a hit record. It sort of happened to me in spite of myself. When I went to California and joined the Navy, I began to sing aboard ship. It helped me build enough confidence to go in front of an audience. What I used to do was listen to the songs of that time, learn the words, and sing for myself. I liked doing it enough that I finally wound up doing it professionally. Eventually, I taught myself an instrument, but I never had any real musical training.

Which instrument was that?

Well, I started off with a set of vibraphones because the group that eventually became known as the Cascades used to be called the Thundernotes. We had this dream that we were going to create this new sound we called "exotic rock." That was when Martin Denny and Arthur Lyman and those people were having top forty hits with records like "Taboo" and "Quiet Village." We were going to take this exotic sound and put it to a rock beat. This was going to be our thing. So they said, "John, you gotta pick up a set of vibes." I went out and rented a set and began by just playing a few chords behind the band. Then every ten minutes or so I'd get up and sing something. The keyboard of the vibes is the same as a piano, so eventually it led me to the electric piano and other keyboard instruments.

Early on, what kind of music were you were listening to?

John Claude Gummoe,
Cleveland, Ohio, 1946

My earliest musical influences were in the fifties with people like Al Martino, Tony Bennett, the Modernaires, and the Hi-Lo's. I love close harmony work. After I left the Cascades, I started another close harmony group called Kentucky Express and we recorded on Cream Records. We tried to model ourselves after Crosby, Stills & Nash, but nothing much ever happened with it. I always admired the Beach Boys, though, always thought they had a great sound. The Lettermen were also just incredible. Then there was the Four Aces, the Four Freshmen, the Everly Brothers, and of course, Johnny Mathis, who always had this incredible voice. But I never was much into Elvis or the Beatles. Not until later when the Beatles did *Abbey Road*.

When did you first feel your music had finally reached some level of success?

When we cut our first record in the summer of '62. We had been performing in clubs in San Diego. I think that was the first time I had a feeling of what it was like to be accepted by an audience. After that, it all happened very quickly. Our second record was "Rhythm of the Rain." Of course, we'd been working together for three years, but when "Rhythm of the Rain" happened it was hard to accept. Certainly we had been working toward it and wanted it badly, but when it actually happened, we didn't really believe it. It took me several months and a few royalty checks before I realized what was happening.

Along the way, was there anyone who was a musical influence for you that you wish you had a chance to spend some time with?

I don't know if this exactly answers the question, but one person I always admired a great deal was Dan Fogelberg. It was so exciting and such a high point for me when he recorded my song. I loved his writing. He was a super, super talent in my eyes. There have been just hundreds of covers of "Rhythm of the Rain," but his is my favorite. He just did a phenomenal job on it. So I went to the Greek Theater to see him perform and I finagled my way backstage to meet him. When I finally did, the first words out of his mouth were, "Well, yeah, the single's doing well, but they pretty much made me put it on the album. They thought it would be a strong single

"When I went to California and joined the Navy, I began to sing aboard ship. It helped me build enough confidence to go in front of an audience."

John Claude Gummoe served in the Navy aboard the USS Jason, AR-8 1958–1962.

because they didn't think anything I had written was good enough." So I'm thinking that's a hell of a thing. Here I'm thanking Dan Fogelberg for doing my song and he's telling me he fought against including it on his album. You know, I would like to have talked to him longer, but the conversation was pretty much over after that. It was kind of a letdown.

Was there anyone along the way who made you feel you weren't on the right path?

I've been very lucky that way. My family and my friends have always been very supportive. I'm a gay man; I've been in a long-term relationship with the same guy for thirty years, and he's always been very supportive. Always right there if something comes up. He goes to the awards dinners with me, whatever. We just have a special relationship. I'm a lucky guy in that respect and I get a lot of support. Since I put up my web site I've been getting e-mail from all over the world and the responses I've gotten have been very moving.

Is there anything you'd like to set straight here for posterity?

"Rhythm of the Rain" was one of the few ballads the Cascades ever did. Maybe it's a small thing, but I'd like people to know we were one "kick-ass" rock group.

Dave Stevens

John Claude Gummoe

The Cascades, 1964

Dave Szabo

Eddy Snyder

Dave Wilson

Disc One
Track 13

Larry Henley on
"The Wind Beneath My Wings"

The Wind Beneath My Wings
Larry Henley and Jeff Silbar

It must have been cold there in my shadow,
To never have sunlight on your face.
You were content to let me shine,
You always walked a step behind.

I was the one with all the glory, while you
Were the one with all the strength.
Only a face without a name,
I never once heard you complain.

Did you ever know that you're my hero,
And everything I would like to be?
I can fly higher than an eagle,
You are the wind beneath my wings.

It might have appeared to go unnoticed,
But I've got it all here in my heart.
I want you to know I know the truth,
I would be nothing without you.

Did you ever know that you're my hero,
And everything I would like to be?
I can fly higher than an eagle,
You are the wind beneath my wings.

You are the wind beneath my wings.

Chapter 12

Larry Henley/Jeff Silbar

PHOTO: TOM BERENS

"Wind Beneath My Wings"

It must have been cold there in my shadow,
To never have sunlight on your face.
You've been content to let me shine,
You always walked a step behind.

I was the one with all the glory
while you were the one with all the strength.
Only a face without a name,
But I never once heard you complain.

Did you ever know that you're my hero.
And everything I'd like to be?
I can fly higher than an eagle,
You are the wind beneath my wings.

It might have appeared to go unnoticed,
But I've got it all here in my heart.
I want you to know I know the truth,
I would be nothing without you.

Did you ever know that you're my hero.
And everything I'd like to be?
I can fly higher than an eagle,
You are the wind beneath my wings.

Larry Henley   *Jeff Silbar*

Larry Henley (left) and Jeff Silbar with their 1990 Grammy Awards for "The Wind Beneath My Wings"

"I don't think it's a songwriter's duty to tell people what to do. I think instead it's to remind people of what they already know." —Larry Henley

Bette Midler

PHOTO: MICHAEL OCHS ARCHIVES.COM

"The Wind Beneath My Wings," written by Larry Henley and Jeff Silbar, was recorded by Bette Midler for Atlantic Records in 1989. It was on Billboard's Hot 100 *for fifteen weeks and hit #1 earning a gold record. It was featured on the soundtrack of* Beaches *and went on to win a Grammy Award for Record of the Year and Song of the Year. "The Wind Beneath My Wings" ranks forty-first on the BMI Top 100 Songs list and has reached more than five million broadcast performances. Larry Henley lives in Nashville, Tennessee, and Jeff Silbar lives in Los Angeles, California.*

The following are excerpts from an interview with Larry Henley.

I was born in Arp, Texas, a long time ago. My mother was a country singer. She started out when she was fourteen, fifteen years old doing radio shows with people like Cowboy Copas, Cowboy Slim Reinhart, and I think she also worked with Ernest Tubb for a time. I liked a lot of the music she introduced me to, like the Nat King Cole Trio, Sarah Vaughn, and Nancy Wilson.

Was there someone early on in your career whom you wanted to succeed for?

I don't know if anybody even understood how much I wanted to succeed and how important it was to me because I was pretty shy as a child and didn't share my feelings too much. I met one of the greatest guys that was ever in my life when I first started out singing with a band. I wasn't making very much money at the time so I didn't even have any decent clothes to wear when I was onstage. This guy came out to see me after the show and told me he was a tailor. He wanted me to come down to his shop so he could make me some suits. I said, "I can't afford any suits," and he said, "Well, we'll worry about the paying for them later." So, he made me some beautiful suits to wear on the stage. Real sharp-looking stuff. Funny, but I think those suits lifted my self-esteem some, so that I wasn't as afraid as I might have been if I hadn't been dressed so nice. Unfortunately, the guy died soon after that so I never got to tell him how much what he had done meant to me. I've always regretted that.

Was there any one big break that opened a lot of doors for you?

I started out working in clubs in Bossier City, Louisiana. It was a little bitty area like the Las Vegas strip in a miniature fashion. They had nightclubs with neon signs on them all up and down the strip. I started off in a place called the Diamond Head Lounge, which was the probably the hottest place on the strip at that time, with a band of mine called the New Beats. This was in the sixties. The New Beats had a hit with a song called "Bread and Butter," which was a #1 hit all around the world, actually. We went on performing for about, I guess, five or six years. I finally quit the group, mainly because I didn't want to sing falsetto the rest of my life.

When you finished recording "Bread and Butter," did you have any idea it would become such a phenomenon?

Since it was my first hit I didn't know what to expect. I will say everyone in the studio thought it had a good chance of being a hit because it was so unique and all. We were all pretty excited. Of course, I was excited about every record I put out in those days. It was one of those crazy records that just took off. One time I pulled into a service station and I was pumping gas and it started playing on the radio. I was looking around for anybody who looked like they liked it. I went up to this girl sitting in a car and said, "That's me!" She looked at me like, "If that's you, what are you doing in a service station pumping gas?" "Bread and Butter" was an overnight success. In those days, to sell 250,000 records in the first week was pretty much unheard of, and still is. I was also shocked over the royalties. We didn't have a very good deal at all, but I was so excited about being a star at that time that I didn't let it bother me too much. Later, I grew to realize what a really lousy deal we had. What little money I did get went to paying off the tabs I had rung up just getting to that point. There were a lot of good people in Bossier City who helped me, fed me, gave me a place to live, and bought my clothes. It was pretty amazing.

Jeff Silbar, Bette Midler, and Larry Henley at the 1990 Grammy Awards

PHOTO: JIM McHUGH
THE RECORDING ACADEMY ©1990

Has there been anybody in the business you've admired but never got a chance to meet?

I guess I'd go back to somebody like Johnny Mercer since he was a big influence on my life. I think I learned a lot from him. I would have liked to have met him and maybe have gotten to write a song with him. That would have been wonderful. But I have met several of my heroes; I met Sam Cooke and I met Marvin Gaye, and those are really my heroes. I got to tell those guys how much I loved their music and all that kind of stuff. I had lunch with Sam Cooke about two weeks before he died. I loved that guy. He was probably the greatest influence on me of all.

Did anyone ever try and talk you out of being in the music business?

Eveybody. I used to work in Louisiana for McCullough Tool Company out in the oil fields, a job I had gotten right out of college. I used to go out with my boss at night and get up and sing with whatever band was playing, if they would let me. My boss would tell me all the time, "You know, you ought to be a singer. What are you doing here in the oil field?" So when I got offered my first singing job, he was the first one I went to tell. And all he did was look at me and say, "Are you crazy? Have you lost your mind?" He was the very guy who had been encouraging me all along. But I never had to ask him for my job back.

Where do you find your inspiration for songwriting?

Life itself, things I see other people do, things that I recognize about what goes on in the world, or even what I think love is. There's all kinds of ways to write a song. You can make them up or you can manufacture them. But if you've got a big enough heart you ought to be a great songwriter.

What were the easiest and the hardest songs that you've written?

To tell you the truth, the easiest may have been "The Wind Beneath My Wings," honestly. Of course, it's something I had in my mind for years. I had the title written down right there in my songbook and the day that Jeff [Silbar] and I got together, we saw that title and that's what we decided to write. It just came out perfect. I was shocked that everybody understood it because it was so poetic. Once I saw it was being accepted, well, that meant a lot to me. I learned a lot from that experience.

Do you think the song appearing in the film Beaches *gave it additional weight and meaning?*

Larry Henley

There was an old movie called *Imitation of Life* with Lana Turner and I forget now who all else was in it. In a funeral scene at the end of the movie, Mahalia Jackson sang some gospel song or other, and I can't remember the title, but it was the most emotional moment I had ever seen in a movie. I'm sure the song itself didn't have as much emotional quality but together with what was on the screen, it just tugged your heart out and had everyone in the movie theater crying. I'll never forget that. As a songwriter I've always dreamed of having a song in a spot like that and lo and behold, it was just exactly what happened with "The Wind Beneath My Wings" and *Beaches*. Seeing it for the first time was probably one of the most exciting moments of my life. I think the song gave to the movie equally as much as the movie gave to the song, if you want to know the truth.

Do feel that the songwriter has a responsibility to his audience more than just to entertain?

I don't think you should preach in a song, but I think you have an obligation to tell the truth, whatever that truth is. I don't think it's a songwriter's duty to tell people what to do. I think instead it's to remind people of what they already know.

The following are excerpts from an interview with Jeff Silbar.

I was born in Key West, Florida, in 1954. We moved around a lot when I was young, but my first real memories are of Lexington, Kentucky, where I went to high school and college. At about the age of thirteen or fourteen, I was playing the guitar and was probably in my first band and writing songs by sixteen. Around my junior year of college, my parents saw that I was so into music that they supported me when I decided to go to Nashville for the summer to see if I could get a job in the music business. I didn't go back to school that fall, I just sort of hung around trying to find my way. I found a job as a runner for Tree Publishing Company and that kind of set the wheels in motion as far as my music career was concerned, since I was learning how to engineer and plug songs. But I wasn't really concentrating on my writing.

Who influenced you to pick up the guitar in your teens?

Ricky Nelson would probably be one of my earliest memories. After that I started getting more into the blues with B.B. King, Albert King and later there was Cream and Led Zeppelin. I also had a love for Hank Williams. Willie [Nelson] and Waylon [Jennings]. They had a kind of rock edge to their music that made me believe there was something for me in Nashville. At that time, Tree Publishing Company was still privately owned and they had some of the all-time great songwriters like Harlan Howard, Hank Cochran, Curly Putman, Willie Nelson, and Bobby Braddock. John Hiatt was also just starting out there at that time. I was working in their demo studio and I got a chance to hear all of them. They'd come into the studio and put their songs down on guitar or piano and then about once or twice a month, there would be a demo session. Being around all that great talent, I got a feel for recognizing a great song. Larry Henley was also writing there at the time so I knew Larry, but like I said, I wasn't songwriting then.

I became a "song plugger." Song plugging was quite a bit different in Nashville than it is now. If you had a great song, you could pretty much call a producer, right up until the time of the downbeat of the recording session. They did their arrangements on the spot and I got a lot of song cuts as a publisher back then.

When did you first feel you were having some success as a writer?

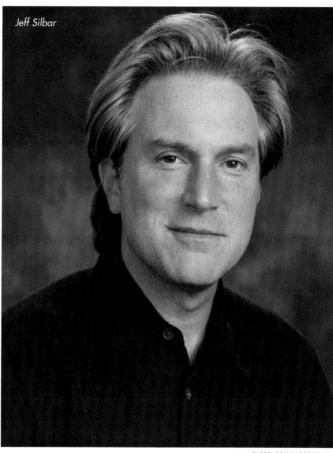

Jeff Silbar

PHOTO: DON HAGOPIAN

I had a songwriting neighbor named Sam Lorber and we made a deal that if we were going to write together the song wouldn't be done until I said it was done. I knew how good it would have to be if I was going to compete with the great writers I had been working around at that time. The first songs Sam and I wrote together were, "Sleep Tight, Goodnight Man" and "Come to My Love." We recorded the songs at the end of a demo session that I was producing for our other writers at House of Gold Music. I dropped one of them off at a Kenny Rogers session on a Friday. On Saturday, I got a phone call saying he'd recorded "Sleep Tight, Goodnight Man," which is on *The Gambler* album that went on to sell millions of records. That was my first real success. The second song, "Come to My Love," became a hit with a singer named Christy Lane. The third song Sam and I had written called "Where Were You When I Was Falling in Love," went on to be a #1 adult contemporary record, for Lobo.

What comes first for you, the lyrics or the melody?

When I have a title, then I feel I'm on to something. It's the heart of the idea. Without it I'm still fishing. I don't think it's a uniquely Nashville thing; it's just a part of the craft of writing. I'll bet most of the great pop songs began with the title.

Would you say songwriting is 99 percent inspiration and 1 percent perspiration or the other way around?

With me, it's the other way around, especially after twenty-five or thirty years of doing it. If I just waited for inspiration, I'd starve. I can think of a number of songs that if we hadn't stuck with them, well, those songs never would have happened. Then there are some other ones that are just gifts.

If you were going to be your worst critic what would you say your strong points and weaknesses are?

My strongest point is also my weakest point, and that is I collaborate when I write. Because of that, I've written with everyone, big ones and small ones. I feel I can pull the best out of them as well as focus. On the other hand, my biggest frustration, my biggest weakness is I find it hard to write on my own. I've always had such amazing respect for someone who can sit there by himself and create beautiful songs and fabulous music. It's a lonely place for me and I've not been able to do it consistently.

Do you have any advice for aspiring songwriters?

From the perspective of both a publisher and a songwriter I'd have to say be patient, and concentrate on getting better. You can waste a lot of time trying to break down doors, but when the time is right, the doors will open for you.

Disc Two
Track 1

John Lee Hooker on
"Boom Boom"

Boom Boom

John Lee Hooker

Boom, boom, boom, boom!
Gonna shoot you right down.
Take me in your arms,
I'm in love with you.
Love that is true.
Boom, boom, boom, boom!

I like the way you walk,
I like the way you talk.
When you walk that walk
And you talk that talk,
You knock me out,
Right off-a my feet.

The way you walk,
The way you talk,
When you walk that walk,
When you talk that talk,
You knock me out.
Right off-a my feet.

I need you right now,
I mean right now,
I don't mean tomorrow,
I mean right now.
Come on, come on,
Come on, shake it up, baby.

Chapter 13

John Lee Hooker

PHOTO: ©EBET ROBERTS
CHANSLEY ENTERTAINMENT ARCHIVES

JOHNLHOOK

BOOM!
BOOM

GUITAR

JOHNLHOOK

"If you didn't have a home, you could come live with my father. If you didn't have food you could come and get yourself fed. If your dog was locked out of the house and didn't have anywhere to go, he could come and live with my father. . . . That was just who he was."

"There was always a sadness in my father's eyes. I loved his eyes. He could look at you with those eyes and tell everything that was going on with you." —Zakiya Hooker-Bell

John Lee Hooker

"Boom Boom" was written and recorded by John Lee Hooker for Vee-Jay Records in 1962. It was on Billboard's Hot 100 for ten weeks and peaked at #60. At the same time, it appeared on Billboard's Rhythm and Blues chart for eight weeks, peaking at #16. A Grammy Award–winning artist, John Lee Hooker was a prolific songwriter with over nine hundred published songs to his credit. This legendary and revered bluesman was inducted into the Rock and Roll Hall of Fame in 1991 and received the Lifetime Achievement Award from the Rhythm and Blues Foundation in 1999. John Lee Hooker died in San Francisco, California, on June 21, 2001.

The following is taken from Bonnie Raitt's speech during the presentation event for John Lee Hooker's induction into the Rock and Roll Hall of Fame in 1991.

"They estimate that between 1949 and 1953 alone, John Lee Hooker had seventy-four singles on twenty-four different labels using twelve names. He recorded over one hundred albums, and when R&B took a backseat to rock and roll in the sixties, he re-created himself as a folk artist and still maintained a success (which is where I heard of him) only to have reemerged as the king of boogie in the seventies. The Canned Heat, the Animals, and everybody else were having hits with his songs. This brings me to one of the things that I think was so different about John Lee and what was so extraordinary about the man and his career: the fact that he avoided at least three pitfalls that are so common to rhythm and blues and rock and roll that it is hard to imagine a career without at least one. First was the fact that he managed to stay successful throughout the whole five decades of his career—something Sinatra may have pulled off, but something extremely rare in our end of the business. Another was that, unlike most of the R&B performers of his era, he actually had copies of his contracts and had collected royalties off his early songs and recordings, and that was a first. The third was that at his age, he was active and making music, not just coasting. I love you, John Lee. You taught me I could get into and out of the blues alive. You were my pal."—Bonnie Raitt

The following are excerpts from an interview with Zakiya Hooker-Bell, John Lee Hooker's daughter.

Is it true that your father was born in Clarksdale, Mississippi, on August 22, 1917?

My mom always said the year was 1912. People say my dad was eighty-four, eighty-five years old, but I'd venture to say he was closer to eighty-seven, eighty-eight. He was pretty up there.

Being a performer, was he concerned about his age?

Yes, he was. When he was younger, I don't think age really bothered him a whole lot, but as he got older, it did. One time, a newspaper kept him at about seventy-five for three years, and then after that, they kept him at eighty for two years. So, as far as the history books are concerned and so on, I'd say he was eighty-five.

Was it in 1943 that your family moved to Detroit?

As far as I know, yes. But in truth, I don't really know. I was born in 1948.

Wasn't that the same year he had a #1 single on the rhythm and blues charts?

That was "Boogie Chillen."

If one looks at your father's discography and the things he accomplished in his lifetime, it's pretty extraordinary.

He was a very gifted man. You know, my dad could neither read nor write, and for him to accomplish what he did back in those early days was simply incredible.

Why was it that in the fifties and sixties, he used such a variety of different names, like Texas Slim, Delta John, Birmingham Sam, and Johnny Williams?

It was so he could record. You know, he didn't understand the "business" of music. Playing music was all he ever wanted to do, and people would try and take advantage of him because he couldn't read or write. They'd simply say, "Sign this contract," or "If you do this we'll pay you that." And, of course, he would because he had eight children that needed to be taken care of.

So he changed names so he could keep recording? In other words, while John Lee Hooker may have signed an exclusive contract with a record company, Texas Slim or Birmingham Sam hadn't, so he was free to also record under those other names?

That's exactly right.

Playing at the 3 Twisted Sister Club, Manchester, England, 1964

PHOTO: ©BRIAN SMITH/
CHANSLEY ENTERTAINMENT ARCHIVES

It's easy to see your father as a true American musical legend, but what kind of a dad was he?

He was a good father and a good provider. We had some rough times, but when he was able to be there, he was always there for us.

Was being on the road a big part of his life at that time?

Yes, it was. When I was a child, and I mean very, very small, being "on the road" didn't mean being out of the country. I think he was pretty much just in the clubs in and around the Detroit area. After "Boogie Chillen," I can remember him going to different countries, and he'd be gone for months on end.

Was it hard to keep in contact with him throughout all that?

PHOTO: CHANSLEY
ENTERTAINMENT ARCHIVES

It was hard on us, in a sense, because he wasn't there. But my father was quite the comedian, even back then. He would sit us around him and tell us old stories that I'm sure he himself had heard as a child. He just always seemed to have a joke to tell, or a story to tell that would keep you laughing. People who knew him well were always saying, "John, you're in the wrong profession. You should have been a comedian." He was a very funny man. When he went out on the road, though, and was gone for any length of time, he'd always bring gifts back with him for all of us. Just to have him back home was a gift. One year, all of us chipped in and bought him this reclining chair for Christmas. He'd give us our presents, and then it was time to get into that recliner. He'd kick back with a cup of coffee and a cigarette and watch baseball. He loved baseball. When he was home he was a complete father.

What was his team?

My daddy's always been a Dodger fan. Dodger blue.

Did he ever go to the games?

My father went to one game as an invited guest of the Dodgers. Oh, he loved that.

What is one of your favorite stories your father told you as a kid?

Back there in the south where my momma and daddy came from they really believed in what's called "hoodoo." We may call it voodoo, but my daddy called it hoodoo. He had a name for everything. He'd tell us a story about this person called Crawlin' Charlie. If you had somebody put a hoodoo spell on you, you could go to Crawlin' Charlie and he would take it off. I used to think this was somebody my daddy just made up. But as we got older I said, "Daddy, why do you keep talking about Crawlin' Charlie? You know he's not real." And he'd say, "Yes, he is. He lived down in the bayou and he couldn't walk, so all he could do was just crawl around." He would say people would travel for miles just to get to Crawlin' Charlie and have their hoodoo undone. And you know, I never knew whether my daddy was pulling our leg or not.

Did he ever use those stories in his music that you know of?

I'm sure some of those stories went into his songs, but for the most part my dad wrote from his own experiences. He might hear an expression, or remember some little something that happened, and then he would write a whole song about it.

Did he run into much racial prejudice?

He used to tell us that when they went to the clubs to play, they'd be able to play but then after they'd have to go in the back door to get their food. Or, they'd play in some hotel, but they weren't allowed to stay there so they'd have to find a place in the black section of town. You know, just those regular stories about what most of the black musicians back then would run into. You could always look in my father's eyes and just know there was so much in there that was not put out there for the world to know. There was always a sadness in my father's eyes. I loved his eyes. He could look at you with those eyes and tell everything that was going on with you. And no matter what you would say, he could see through to what was really going on. He always knew. You could never go to him and tell a lie. He just always knew; those eyes were like deep, deep, pools. I loved his eyes; I loved his hands. There were times I was content to say nothing; just sit there and look at him.

In his sixties, seventies, and into his eighties, so many rock musicians paid homage to him—Eric Clapton, Carlos Santana, Van Morrison, Bonnie Raitt, Mick Jagger, Keith Richards, and many more. Was he surprised?

Y ou know, he's always been my hero, so I could understand why he was everyone else's hero. I think they even felt the power that he generated. It was like, "If I could only just get to him and touch him, then maybe I can get some of it and absorb it." My father loved people. At the memorial service, my brother got up and was talking about my dad and said, "If you didn't have a home, you could come live with my father. If you didn't have food you could come and get yourself fed. If your dog was locked out of the house and didn't have anywhere to go, he could come and live with my father." My father just took people in and he asked nothing in return. That was just who he was.

Were you ever around when these musicians came to visit with him?

A lot of times the visits happened in the studios. Out of all of them, Bonnie [Raitt] was the one who would come and visit and always stayed in touch with him. You know, I think he became like another father to her.

Is there anything people don't know about your father that isn't out there in the tributes and the biographies that you might want them to know?

I suppose it would be that even though my father couldn't read and couldn't write, he was truly one of the wisest men that I have ever known. There's a line in a song that says, "Educated into a fool" and that's where a lot of people wind up. They think that just because you can't read and you can't write, that you don't have the capability to deal with what's going on around you. Back in the early days my father was really taken advantage of, and I'd like those people to know he knew what was going on. He may not have acted on it, and he may have let it go by, but he understood when people were using him, when people were honest, and when people were truly his friends. He had the kind of common sense that transcends all the books in the world. He was a realist and even tried to prepare all of us for his leaving. But then there came a point when he said, "I got to go."

We were talking one day toward the end and he said, "You know, I had a dream the other night. I dreamed I was in heaven and I saw all of my old friends. I saw Muddy [Waters] and I saw Howlin' Wolf. I saw Albert Collins and Albert King, and we were all up there together and there was a big band and everybody was just up." He said it was beautiful and he said he would be there pretty soon. And I told him I didn't want to talk about it. He said, "You have to talk about it because I'm not going to live forever. You have to prepare yourself for that. And I don't want no hootin' and hollerin' and cryin' when I go out. I want to have a party." So that's what I gave him. I gave him his party. My daddy especially didn't like snakes and worms. He'd always say, "Snakes and worms, they're all in the ground, and those worms, they'll eat you up." He didn't want to be cremated so I had him entombed in a beautiful place called the Chapel of Chimes here in Oakland, California. Julia Morgan designed a beautiful building which has an inside garden with atriums, skylights, and fountains. He'd have loved it because it's quiet, but he'd also have loved it because he's above ground.

Disc Two
Track 2

Jessi Colter on
"Good Hearted Woman"

Good Hearted Woman

Willie Nelson and Waylon Jennings

A long time forgotten are dreams that just fell by the way
And the good life he promised ain't what she's livin' today,
But she never complains of the bad times or the bad things he's done Lord
She just talks about the good times they've had and all the good times to come.

She's a good hearted woman in love with a good timin' man.
She loves him in spite of his ways that she don't understand.
Through teardrops and laughter they'll pass through this world hand in hand.
A good hearted woman lovin' her good timin' man.

He likes the night life, the bright lights and good timin' friends.
When the party's all over she'll welcome him back home again.
Lord knows she don't understand him, but she does the best that she can.
'Cause she's a good hearted woman she loves her good timin' man.

She's a good-hearted woman in love with a good timin' man.
She loves him inspite of his ways that she don't understand.
Through teardrops and laughter, they'll pass through this world hand in hand.
A good hearted woman lovin' her good timin' man.

Chapter 14

Waylon Jennings

PHOTO COURTESY OF SHOWTIME MUSIC
ARCHIVES (TORONTO)/PICTORIAL PRESS

"Good Hearted Woman"

a Long Time forgotten
    are dreams that Just fell By The Way
The good life he promised
    Aint What she's livin' To day
But she Never complains
    Of The bad Times or the bad Thing he's done - Lord
She just Talks about The Good Times
    They've had-y all The good Times To come

Cho:

    She's a good hearted Woman
        In love with a good Timin' Man
    She loves him inspite of his ways
        That she don't understand
Through Teardrop & Laughter
    They'll pass Through This World hand in hand
A good hearTed Woman
    lovin' her good Timin' Man

He likes The Night life. The bright lights
    and good Timin' friends
When The ParTy's all over
    She'll welcome him back home again
Lord Knows she don't understand him
    But she does The best That she can
This good hearTed Woman
    lovin' her good Timin' Man

Cho:

"He was born and raised in West Texas, which had a river of music history running through it. He would often say the reason he thought music was so important in Texas was because it wasn't manufactured. It was something the everyday hard-working people were playing themselves."

"Everything he did was in spite of something else. He was an original. Everything he did was original and that was just part of the price he paid." —Jessi Colter

Waylon Jennings

"Good Hearted Woman," written by Waylon Jennings and Willie Nelson, was recorded by Waylon Jennings for RCA Records in 1972. Topping the country charts, his recording received a Grammy nomination for Best Country Vocal Performance, Male. When Waylon teamed with Willie Nelson in 1976, "Good Hearted Woman," landed again on Billboard's Top 40 *for five weeks and won both artists Country Music Awards for Single of the Year and for Vocal Duo of the Year. Waylon Jennings was inducted into the Nashville Songwriters Hall of Fame in 1995 and the Country Music Hall of Fame in 2001. Born in Littlefield, Texas, he died at his home in Chandler, Arizona, on February 13, 2002, at the age of sixty-four.*

The following are excerpts from an interview with Waylon Jennings's wife, Jessi Colter.

It's known that Waylon grew up desperately poor. Did that circumstance motivate him at all?

Waylon had a lot of little boy traits that remained with him his whole life through and were very charming, but he had been forced to become a man very early on, working in those West Texas cotton fields. And yet despite the land he lived on and the terrible conditions he endured, these circumstances all contributed to a survival strength in him that was amazing.

Do you think there was any reason for his broad-ranging taste in music?

He was born and raised in West Texas, which had a river of music history running through it. He would often say the reason he thought music was so important in Texas was because it wasn't manufactured. It was something the everyday hard-working people were playing themselves. Everywhere you went in West Texas, music poured out of the screen doors and porches of every house you passed. There was a guitar, piano, or fiddle in just about every home. It's just what they did at the end of the day to raise themselves up out of the dust. Waylon was there, and he was listening, just devouring everything there was to be heard. And from the very beginning he knew what he liked. He heard all of it, bluegrass, country, R&B, rock and roll, just all of it. He gravitated toward rhythm. Very few people know that his favorite song ever recorded was Bob Seger's "Katmandu." As a teenager, Buddy Holly was an influence too. He could see what was going on with Buddy right after Elvis Presley. And then, of course, came the Beatles. We're talking about standing by the cradle of rock and roll, and the transformation of country music, and Waylon was there listening to it all. Jonathan Yardley of the *Washington Post*, in reviewing Waylon's autobiography, wrote, "I don't know how this man who just got his GED has done it, but he's managed to write the most comprehensive view of the American popular music business that's ever been written. It's something you should read for the history of the business even if you don't care for the man or his music." I just think Waylon's musical sensibilities were shaped by the circumstances of his life, and the time and the place where he was born and raised.

The idea of Waylon as the "outlaw" was very powerful to his fans, but was that the way he saw himself?

Waylon Jennings, 1985

He didn't create that image. He didn't pose or portray anything, he just was who he was. In 1968, he was thirty-two years old and had worked since he was twelve or fourteen. What he saw going on in Nashville at that time—how the artist was treated, or mistreated to be honest—was so incredulous compared with the rest of the world. I think what happened next came from great creative frustration. Waylon finally had to put his foot down and say, "I'm going to take a risk here, a very big gamble, and I'll either win or lose it all." That's when he cut his *Honky Tonk Heroes* album. Waylon had a major creative run-in with the producer on staff and so he was forced to engineer—to completely build the album from nothing. He felt that he had served his time and paid his dues; he'd been an intern for long enough. In fact, he was much more creative and productive than anyone he was surrounded by and so he took the reins into his own hands. Of course, it was against the better judgment of everyone he was working with and totally against what was acceptable in Nashville at the time. But it was something he had seen done all the time in L.A. and New York. It had just never been tried before in Nashville because the "old guard" was very powerful and very strong. I guess this is the long way of saying he didn't envisage himself as an "outsider" or an "outlaw"; he just found himself in that position in order to express himself creatively. From day one he had a vision of who he was, and what he could accomplish. That's just who Waylon was.

You married in 1969. For a while, it was a pretty lean time professionally until the phenomenal recognition of his album Honky Tonk Heroes. *What was that time like?*

PHOTO: ©EBET ROBERTS/CHANSLEY ENTERTAINMENT ARCHIVES

It was a great struggle and, of course, in 1970, he became very ill. He had to lay down for an entire month and then had to ask for an advance from RCA, who only offered him a pittance. That's when Neil Reshen, our manager, came into the picture. He knew how to handle the big corporations and began to avenge Waylon, businesswise. It was a quite a long struggle but a very exciting one. But yes, it was a struggle. I was young and so fascinated with Waylon and his life. It was great fun being with him and sharing his life. From day one it was such a joy being on the sideline just listening to him sing. But it was a struggle. I was twenty-five and he was thirty-two. I inherited his five children—three of them came to live with us. I had a daughter as well. In those years, he was driven to work to cover the alimony and his problems of the past, and his children had already been pretty much affected by the bitterness of the women involved. I wish that somebody had given me a book, but life doesn't come with an instruction manual, does it? I wanted to be supportive of Waylon, and do everything I could, because he was a force in our culture. He was revolutionary in country music, with good reason, because he loved making music.

Did he feel he was constantly pushing the stone uphill?

He had to feel that way because it was true. Everything he did was in spite of something else. He was an original. Everything he did was original and that was just part of the price he paid.

It's been said Waylon was remarkably in touch with his audience. Where did that come from, and where did he find his inspiration?

He just had something in him that read people. He could feel those people and what they needed. Often artists of his caliber and seniority do for themselves, or just what they want to do. Waylon did things for his people, his audience. He wanted to make things so plain and believable that he wouldn't lose them. He was a great, great communicator. There's no other way to define it. He didn't go about it in any self-conscious way. He was a bit of a doctor; somebody who could just walk into a room and know whether a person was hurting or needing something. He always would make a place for children. I've never seen anyone else like him as far as that goes. He had an incredible heart.

Waylon Jennings and Buddy Holly

PHOTO COURTESY OF SHOWTIME MUSIC ARCHIVES (TORONTO)/JIM DAWSON

Was Waylon a natural collaborator or did he prefer to work on his own?

He was a self-starter. He wrote many, many songs on his own, but when it was with the right person, he enjoyed cowriting. He liked to see the reaction of the people who he worked with. I think that was the entertainer in him. He was just so honest. Not all entertainers are.

Did success help him to deal with his personal demons?

Loving him and seeing him for what he was, I can't really say I ever saw those demons. I can't say that he was driven by some great pain or anything like that. I just think he was meant to be who he was. Obviously, God believed he had completed his purpose or he wouldn't have called him away. He loved deeply, but he couldn't talk too seriously for too long. I think it was because he felt things so deeply. He just didn't like to explain it and drain it. He would always leave you wanting more. He just had what he needed to be an incredible musician with a voice, and I don't know of another who can equal it.

Beside yourself, what was his favorite distraction?

Music was his favorite distraction. Even when he was very ill at the end, he was still working, arranging, and thinking about what he should do next. He was looking ahead to some of the music he planned to make. The last two weeks before he crossed on over, he worked with a producer listening to many, many tapes to see what they'd be taking into the studio next. He never stopped. He was always working. He wasn't an outdoors kind of guy, and yet he loved going onto the remote property that belonged to my father. My father had built a little place that was totally self-sufficient. We didn't rely on the electric company, water, or anything. We would just go up there for a week at a time. That was one of his great joys. Anything he set his mind to do, he did well, whether it was golfing, shooting, or whatever. If he wanted to do it, you best not even mess with him. But if he didn't want to do it, then you best not even mess with him. Another distraction, if you could call it that, was messing with people. If he could get a group of people together and hold court, just get them to laughing, that made his day.

Did being so ill give him a different perspective?

It did. Long ago he turned away from drugs, and from that time on he just wanted to be a straight arrow. He made that happen. He gained a broader and even deeper sense of the eternal things that mattered at the end. There was a transformation—a metamorphosis going on inside of him that, if there had been more time, would have produced some new and exciting things, had that been the call.

What do you think he was most proud of?

I think he was most proud of the fact that he never forgot those who were hurting or in need. He never talked much about receiving the Horatio Alger Award that Johnny Cash nominated him for. He didn't really want for people to talk about his humanitarian accomplishments. For instance, something I just learned recently was that he loved to travel down to the Galloping Goose, which was one of he very first clubs he ever worked at. It's in Coolidge, Arizona, which is a town that's so depressed I don't even know how it still stands. He liked to show people where he started out from, which was such a far cry from where he ended up. We went down not long before he passed away and there on a wall, in the club, was a newspaper clipping about one of his first concerts there. He wasn't but nineteen then and this article in this yellowing local paper mentioned that he had done a

benefit for a woman who had just lost her child. That's just not the usual thing you do at nineteen. But it's only one of the many small things you could find out about him that he'd like to keep to himself. Awards and things like that made him uncomfortable. He really did believe in giving and not talking too much about it, which of course, was Christ's way. The second thing he would be most proud of is that he really did change the country music business, did turn it around, and opened the door for other people. He was most proud of being a good father to our son, Shooter, and most proud of our marriage. He held it very dear because we had been through a lot together.

Was there anything he might have felt was left unfinished?

When he first had congestive heart failure, he was so ill he could hardly breathe or move and we pretty much retired from the hard push of work for eighteen months. Aside from being sick, it also just bored him stupid, and he said, "I'll just not ever do that again." He was always thinking of music. I can't speak for him or say he left anything unfinished. He wrote an incredible book of his life story that I am so proud of, and also because he turned down an offer for twice as much for it if he would have been willing to make it "sensational." It's a true piece of history, not just about Waylon but about the evolution of this business.

Did Waylon as "the outsider" really know how highly regarded he was?

You know, he had a good time when we traveled out here one winter. He put all his things on cassettes to listen to in the car. The ones that had been done well along with a few new things that hadn't yet seen the light of day. It was a sort of self-compiled retrospective. And on that long drive, the two of us listened to all of it as we traveled. He said, "You know, all these years I've been recording, I've been working so hard to get this stuff out, I've never really sat down and just listened—listened the way somebody might who's just gone out and bought an album." I think at that moment he did have a sense that he was appreciated, remembered, and well thought of in his field.

A Dylan Thomas poem has a line that goes something like "Do not go gentle into that good night." In the end, did Waylon go gently or did he fight to the last?

He did go gently in the end, but he also fought it for a time—you know, like you fight sleep. He did want to live and had a very celebrated sense of life. And he did not lay down easy. It just speaks of his great courage and sense of life, because most men would have laid down two years earlier. Just laid down and given up. We all have to pass through this door. In my thinking, if I can only fight half as valiantly as he fought, I will have achieved something. It's a testament to him and a great legacy.

"He just didn't like to explain it and drain it. He would always leave you wanting more."

PHOTO: ©EBET ROBERTS/
CHANSLEY ENTERTAINMENT ARCHIVES

Merle Kilgore on
"Ring of Fire"

Ring of Fire
Merle Kilgore and June Carter

Love, is a burning thing
And it makes a fiery ring
Bound, by wild desires
I fell into a Ring of Fire

I fell into a burning Ring of Fire
I went down, down, down
And the flames went higher
And it burns, burns, burns
The Ring of Fire, The Ring of Fire

The taste, of love is sweet
When hearts, like ours meet
I fell for you like a child
Oh . . . but the fire went wild

I fell into a burning Ring of Fire
I went down, down, down
And the flames went higher
And it burns, burns, burns
The Ring of Fire, The Ring of Fire

Chapter 15

Merle Kilgore

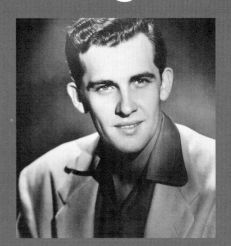

"Ring of Fire"

Love, is a Burning thing
And it makes, a firey ring
Bound, by wild Desire
I fall into a Ring of Fire

cho. I fall into a Burning Ring of Fire
I want Down, Down, Down,
And The Flames want Higher
And it Burns, Burns, Burns,
The Ring of Fire, the Ring of Fire

The taste, of love is sweet
When Hearts, like ours meet
I fell for you Like a child
Oh--- But the Fire Went Wild

June Carter
Merle Kilgore

"One day, I got up the courage to ask one of the musicians, 'How do you get into show business? I think this is what I wanna do.' He took a long drag on his cigarette, blew smoke in my face and said, 'Hang out with sombody famous, kid.'"

"So I asked Hank Williams, 'Why are you reading all them sissy True Romance Comic Books?'" He said right back at me, 'Sissy, hell. Where do you think I get my ideas from, boy?'"

Johnny Cash

"Ring of Fire," written by Merle Kilgore and June Carter, was recorded by Johnny Cash for Columbia Records in 1963. This song was #1 on Billboard's Country Singles *chart for seven weeks, peaked at #17 on* Billboard's Hot 100, *and earned a gold record. It went on to win a CMR Award for Best Song of the Year and received a Grammy nomination for Best Country Western Recording. That same year, Merle Kilgore was named a* Billboard *Top Ten Songwriter of the Year. Johnny Cash's recording of "Ring of Fire" was inducted into the Grammy Hall of Fame in 1998. Merle Kilgore was inducted into the Nashville Songwriters Hall of Fame in 1998 and lives in Paris, Tennessee.*

I was born in Chickasha, Oklahoma, on August 9, 1934. My father was a federal agent and the U.S. government sent him to to Louisiana after Huey Long, who he never was able to collar. The family moved to Shreveport when I was three years old. So I'm an Okie, but I was raised in Louisiana. Musically speaking, the most important place to have born in the U.S. might be Nashville, Tennessee, but Shreveport has to come in a close second. I don't know if it's in the water or the air or what, but Shreveport nurtured the likes of Elvis Presley, Hank Williams, Johnny Cash, Johnny Horton, and the list goes on and on. Right there in Shreveport was a radio station called KWKH, a big "fifty thousand watter" which covered all of Texas and the southwest, all the way to Los Angeles. I was thirteen or fourteen years old when I heard this boy in my school singing one of the Bailes Brothers songs, so I said, "Hey, I didn't know you sang." And he said, "Oh, I sing a little and fool around with a guitar. My daddy books the Bailes Brothers for hospital events and the like. If you want, I'll take you down to the broadcast and you can meet 'em personally." In 1948 in Shreveport, there was no television at all and radio was still king. So I knew I had to go down to where they were broadcasting from and listen in. All we had to do was make ourselves useful by carrying the musicians' instruments up to the station. I guess I went down there just about every Saturday. Pretty soon, I got to bicycle down there nearly every day. There was a little café called Murrell's where all the entertainers hung out for coffee before the station opened up. One day, I got up the courage to ask one

of the musicians, "How do you get into show business? I think this is what I wanna do." He took a big draw on his cigarette, blew smoke in my face, and said, "Hang around with somebody famous, kid."

Soon after, I heard that Hank Williams was coming to the *Louisiana Hayride* and was gonna do the morning radio show. So, me and my friend Ed Knight stood and waited until 5:30 in the morning when here came this big old beat-up Town and Country Chrysler. It had the wood on the doors and was smokin' and rattlin', and I said, "God, Ed, look at that old car." The car stopped and a guy in a white suit and a cowboy hat stepped out, and I said, "Man, that's Hank Williams." We ran across the

Merle Kilgore talking to singer Margie Bowles at radio station WSM in Nashville the night before Merle's first appearance on The Grand Ole Opry in 1960

PHOTO: LES LEVERETT

street. I saw he had his guitar, a briefcase, and a hat in his hands, so I said to him, "Let me carry somethin' for you." I took the guitar and got to ask him a million questions. After a time, I was allowed to go along with him in that big Packard limousine he took to ridin' in to get to the performances. One of those times I saw him reading True Romance Comic Books and I said, "My sister reads True Romance Comic Books." So, I asked Hank Williams, "Why are you reading all them sissy True Romance Comic Books?" He said right back at me, "Sissy, hell. Where do you think I get my ideas from, boy?" He told me he had this little spiral notebook that he kept in his suit pocket and a little bitty pencil stuck in the spiral. "You get an idea, you hear somebody say somethin' funny, write it down. When you write a song you gotta have a title. You hear something that sounds like a title, write it down and work it out from there. That's how I do it. You just can't sit there and make it up. If you wanna make it, you can't fake it; you gotta live it."

When I was eighteen I wrote my first #1, million-seller called "More and More." I sang it on TV and Webb Pierce saw me and said, "That's Merle Kilgore, he used to carry my guitar at the *Hayride*." He called me and he said, "Come on out, son, and have a Christmas drink with me. By the way, that song you sing, 'More and More,' damn, I like that song. Come out here and sing it to me." So that opened a lot of doors for me.

Do you have to wait for inspiration to find you or do you chase after it?

Well, you know, the slow, hard way is to wait for inspiration. And how do you get inspiration? Well, you pop a pill or you take a drink. You just can't have your heart broken in a million pieces all the time. Some of my dear songwritin' friends have never, ever been happy. They are so happy to be unhappy, because they think bein' miserable will help them come up with great titles. So I quit writin' years ago because damn, a guy could kill himself doin' it that way. June Carter and I were working with the Johnny Cash Road Show and June and Johnny were madly in love, but they were both married. See, great songs do come out of misery. One day June said to me, "When we're off the road, we ought to get together and write." So we got together and we started writin'. Hank Snow recorded a song we wrote together called "A Promise to John." Of course, the John referred to in the title is Johnny Cash. Well, June and I would meet two or three times a week and throw ideas around. One day, June said a friend of hers was going through a terrible divorce and she read me a few lines from a letter her friend had written her. She read, "Love is like a burning ring of fire." I said, "Oh yeah, I like that." So we started on the song. Eventually we took it down and sang it to Anita [Carter], who needed another song to complete her album. Later, Johnny heard Anita's recording and said, "Man, I love that song." One day, Johnny sat down to breakfast and told us he had this strange dream. In his dream he heard "Ring of Fire" with Mexican trumpets in it and he was singing it. He told us if Anita's record wasn't a hit, he was going to record it. The rest is history.

Are there any songs you've written that were particularly hard to write?

Oh, yeah. I had a song called "The Folk Singer" which I wrote for Tommy Roe. I was over at Lefty's house. I don't know if you're familiar with Lefty Frizzell, but Lefty and Hank Williams, they set the whole pattern for country music. Anyway, I was working on the song at Lefty's house and he said, "You've been workin' on that song for a whole day. It's not my kinda song, and I'm not gonna record it." So, when I finished after about two hard days of working on it, Milton Jarvis, who had an office

Johnny Cash, Harlan Howard, and Merle Kilgore left in the middle of a rehearsal for an appearance at the Hollywood Bowl in 1962 to do a little fishing.

next door to mine on Music Row, said, "Man, I gotta get this to Tommy Roe. I want him to cut it." So, Tommy cut "The Folk Singer." Eddy Arnold cut it, Jimmy Brown and the Browns cut it, and eight or ten other singers must've covered that song. Tommy had a #1 record in Europe with it. That was the hardest song I ever wrote.

Do you think in words first or music?

Words first. I can go back thirty years, so when my wife gets out the scrapbooks and if I can see my own handwriting, the melody will come back to me just like when I wrote it, without reading the music or nothin'. But if somebody typed out the lyrics and I read it, I wouldn't remember the melody worth a damn. If I see my handwriting the melody comes back, just like that.

Was there anyone early on whom you wanted to succeed for?

Well, you know, I had such a burning desire to be around the great entertainers like Hank Williams. People worshiped Hank Williams and I still do. I saw those diamonds and those Packard limousines and I said, "This is for me. How do you do this?" My father, he was totally against it of course, but he helped me. He said, "Okay, you want a Martin guitar, you get half the money, I'll put up the other half. You want a tape recorder?" Same thing. They were very expensive back then and we got a tape recorder and my dad helped. My folks stood behind me all my career.

When was the first time you heard yourself on the radio?

The song was "More and More." I met with Sonny James, who I knew from the old *Louisiana Hayride* days, and he said, "What's your best song?" and I sang it to him. And he said, "Oh, another crying hillbilly song." Of course he'd been cuttin' a lot of the blues stuff on Imperial [Records], but he really loved country. He said, "Oh, okay, let's put this down." And so my record started gettin' heavy play and Webb Pierce called me and said, "Son, listen I've been thinkin' about your song. Everywhere I go they are talkin' about your record 'More and More.' You give me half of it and I'll make it number one and that'll open the door for your music career." And I said, "Do it." He did it and he was right.

So you cut him in on it?

I gave him half. He was real honest about the deal and he'd say, "Here's a song that Merle Kilgore wrote and I cut myself in for half." He really opened the door for me. The first time I met Elvis Presley he said, "Oh my God, you wrote 'More and

More' and you worked with Hank Williams." And I said, "That's right." So after that, Elvis told his agents, "I want Merle to open shows for me."

Do you have any special routine to get into the mood to write?

I haven't written much in the last fifteen years, 'cause I've been in the management end. People still ask me, "Merle, have you written any hits lately?" I've written a lot of ideas down, a lot of great titles. But with me, if I start a song and I don't finish, it's dead, I can never go back to it. I'd have to call somebody in to help finish it. I haven't had a drink in twenty-five years; but before, I used to have a drink or two to get in a mellow mood and see what I could come up with. Unfortunately, it's one of the things that's destroyed a lot of songwriters, even back to Stephen Foster.

Is there any favorite distraction that gets you to put down the pencil and do something else?

TV. You know, you put the mute button on and then you look up and say, "What the hell is that?" Or, "Oh, God, there's that beautiful girl. Who is she?" TV's the worst invention for writers.

Was there anyone you wanted to, but never got a chance to meet?

Jack Clement's studio, Nashville, 1988

Johnny Cash

Jack Clement

Hank Williams, Jr.

Merle Kilgore

PHOTO: BETH GWINN

God, I've met them all. But I'll tell you what, a guy who I always wanted to meet was Gordon Lightfoot. I'm in the Songwriters Hall of Fame, and they asked me if I would do the Hall of Fame show in Nashville last year. Gordon Lightfoot was on the show and, like I said, I've always wanted to meet him. Let's see, there was Gordon Lightfoot, Donna Summer, me, and the guy who wrote "Ghostbusters," John [Ruttger], what's his name? They told me, "You gotta handle Gordon with kid gloves." I said, "Hey, Hank Williams, Johnny Cash, Hank Williams Jr., I'm the expert on kid gloves, are you kiddin' me? That's a piece of cake." And so, Gordon was in his dressing room while we were all rehearsing. Finally, someone said, "Gordon wants to see you." So I went into his dressing room and he said, "Merle, they want me to sing 'Sundown.'" And I said, "Yeah?" He said, "That song is just too personal to me and I don't wanna sing it." I said, "Well, fuck 'em. Don't sing it then." And he said, "Really, no kiddin'?" "Don't sing it if you don't wanna sing it." And man, Gordon got so happy. He started shakin' hands with everybody and meetin' everybody. Then he said, "Oh, by the way, Merle, before I had any hit songs I used to put 'Wolverton Mountain' [also written by Merle Kilgore] in my set every damn night. I know every word of that song backward. You wanna hear me sing it?" And that's just what he did. That was one of the biggest thrills I've had in a long time.

Do you have some advice for aspiring young songwriters?

The best advice I can give is what Hank Williams told me, "If you wanna make it, you can't fake it, you gotta live it. Get yourself a title. Once you have that, the words and music will come." He also said, "Try and make the melody familiar without crossin' over and makin' it a direct steal—that'll get you in trouble. People like a familiar melody."

*Ben E. King on
"Stand by Me"*

Stand by Me

Jerry Leiber, Mike Stoller, Ben E. King

*When the night has come
And the land is dark
And the moon is the only light we'll see
No I won't be afraid
Oh I won't be afraid
Just as long as you stand
Stand by me.*

*So darling, darling
Stand by me
Oh stand by me*

*Oh stand
Stand by me
Stand by me*

*If the sky that we look upon
Should tumble and fall
Or the mountain should crumble to the sea
I won't cry, I won't cry
No I won't shed a tear
Just as long as you stand, stand by me.*

*And darling, darling
Stand by me
Oh stand by me*

*Oh stand now
Stand by me
Stand by me*

String solo

*Darling darling
Stand by me
Oh stand by me*

*Oh stand now
Stand by me
Stand by me*

*When ever you're in trouble
Won't you stand by me
Oh stand by me
Oh won't you stand now
Oh stand
Stand by me*

Chapter 16

Ben E. King

PHOTO: ©EBET ROBERTS/
CHANSLEY ENTERTAINMENT ARCHIVES

Stand By Me.

When the night has come, and the land is dark
And the Moon is the only light we'll see
No I won't be afraid, No I won't be afraid.
Just as long as you Stand, Stand By Me.
    So darling, darling Stand By me, Oh
Stand By me, Oh Stand, Stand By me
Stand By me.

If the sky that we look upon
Should tumble and fall, or the Mountain
Should crumble to the sea, I won't cry, I
won't cry. No I won't shed a tear.
Just as long as you Stand, Stand By me.
    So darling, darling, Stand By me, Oh
Stand By me, Oh Stand Now, Stand
By me.   Stand By me.

Darling, darling Stand By me, Oh Stand By me
Oh Stand Now.   Stand By me.   Stand By me
When ever you're in trouble won't you Stand
By me, Oh Stand By me, Oh won't you Stand Now.
    Stand By me   Stand By me.

"I would imagine the easiest songs [to write] were the ones I wrote when I was younger, because I didn't really know what writing was all about. I was just writing from my heart and my feelings and simply didn't know any better."

"You'd be walking down the street and hear the whole song playing from storefronts, open windows, and the front stoops everywhere from one end of Harlem to the other."

Ben E. King

PHOTO: ROBERT CORWIN

"Stand by Me" was written by Ben E. King, Jerry Leiber, and Mike Stoller. First recorded by Ben E. King for Atco Records in 1961, it reached the #4 position on Billboard's Hot 100. Certified with over seven and a half million broadcast performances by BMI, the song was also a top twenty hit for John Lennon during his solo career. In 1986, twenty-five years after its initial release, it hit the top of the charts again as the title song for the feature film Stand by Me. *Ben E. King now lives in New Jersey where he oversees the Ben E. King Stand by Me Foundation.*

I was born in Henderson, North Carolina, on September 28, 1938, and like most of us out of the South, started singing in church because that's the place that you found yourself almost seven days of the week. My mother said I was the youngest one in the choir and she's probably right because I was too young to remember.

When you're working on a song, what comes first, the words or the music?

I write mostly lyrics, but I can do what they call "arranging" in my head. I know how to explain to anybody what I want, but I can't write it out. So whenever I start writing a lyric for some reason, I don't know how, but the music seems to just come along with it. Just one of those things I'm blessed with, I guess.

Do you like to collaborate?

Over the last few years, my son Ben Jr. and I have collaborated on a lot of stuff because I've tried to get him involved in the business. He has a knack for it. He plays an instrument and writes well. Over the last five or six years, I started working with other artists, not that my brain wasn't working anymore, but I just found that they were bringing a lot to the table that I could appreciate. I prefer writing alone because once you have that "thing," the song, it's your baby and you don't have to ask nobody's opinion. Otherwise, it's like being married to that particular song with someone else and you're definitely married.

PHOTO: COURTESY WAYNE KNIGHT COLLECTION/
CHANSLEY ENTERTAINMENT ARCHIVES

Is there anything you do to get into a creative mood?

I guess I just let the inspiration find me. I've written songs on napkins in restaurants or overheard people say things and thought, "That would make a good lyric for a song." So I make a note of what they say.

Have some songs been easier to write than others?

I would imagine the easiest songs were ones I wrote when I was younger, because I didn't really know what writing was all about. I was just writing from my heart and my feelings and simply didn't know any better.

Was gospel music a big influence in your life when you were growing up?

Pretty much. I don't remember if we even had a radio. As I remember it, there was only church music and hillbilly music. My daddy liked to listen to that sort of thing, but I didn't pay much attention to it. So church music was about the only music I knew at that time.

When was the first time it struck you that you were having some real success?

Success for me came as sort of an accident. The way I became the lead singer for the new Drifters was because I had written a song and while we were in the studio recording it, the guy who was the lead singer, for some reason or another, couldn't get the lyrics together. So Jerry Wexler, who was the vice president of Atlantic Records at that time, yelled up into the control room, "What's the problem with this song?" The session was being produced by Jerry Leiber and Mike Stoller and one of them told Jerry, "Benny wrote the song, but uh, the lead singer has a problem with it." So Wexler said, "Then let Benny do it, let Benny sing the song." Well, I thought I'd just put it down temporarily until they could find somebody else to sing it. And that's how I became the lead singer for the new Drifters. Up until that

The Drifters, 1959

Charles Thomas

Ben E. King

Doc Green

Elsbeary Hobbs

PHOTO COURTESY OF SHOWTIME MUSIC ARCHIVES (TORONTO)

point, I don't think I ever thought of wanting to be a lead singer. I was enjoying myself just writing and being a background singer and I was having fun with what I was doing. So when it came time that the record was released and I heard it on the radio walking down the street in Harlem, I was floored. When it became a hit, you could have knocked me over.

You mean they were playing it out of the storefronts on the street?

At that time, everybody pretty much listened to just one radio station up in Harlem. So you'd be walking down the street and hear the whole song playing from storefronts, open windows, and the front stoops everywhere from one end of Harlem to the other. Everyone in the neighborhood knew the story of how we had become the new set of Drifters. We kept the name of the

group alive by going out on tour even with no record of our own, just by singing the songs the old Drifters had recorded. We had to keep the name going just to keep the record company behind us. When we finally recorded our first record, we didn't know what would happen even after we had finished it. But as soon as the record came out, we knew it was a wonderful record and we were really, really impressed with what Leiber and Stoller had done with it. On the street, we all got that, "Man, I heard your record," and this and that. It was also one of the first records, from what I was told, to have strings and all that stuff on it. We had kettle drums, violins, cellos, and oboes on there but, of course, none of that was there when we laid down the vocal tracks. Later on, they said we were making history with that particular song.

It must have been clear that you had a runaway hit on your hands. Did you celebrate?

Our first manager lived in Harlem and I think we all went by his place and had some cheap wine or whatever. But the "money" wasn't really there yet, and so we were still hanging in there with the cheap stuff. We never received a check for that first record; there was nothing like that. The way I remember it, the manager who had been with the Drifters before—and I call them the original Drifters—had fired them and hired us. When he hired us to become the "new set" of Drifters, he put us all on salary so we were getting like a hundred and five or ten dollars a week. But there was never a first royalty check. There wasn't any going out and buying a car or anything like that, far from it.

Was there anyone in particular who stood by you in the lean years?

His name was L-O-V-E-R, Lover Patterson—that's what he called himself. I think he thought he was the Romeo of Harlem and he became my first manager. Like I said, we were on salary as the new Drifters. While we were out on tour, one of our guys happened to see one of the contracts for the engagement that night. We were all floored by the amount of money "they" were making and still just paying us a small amount, like a hundred dollars a week. So we decided to get back to New York and have a meeting with the manager. At the meeting, they chose me to be the one to stand up and talk, which I did. The manager said that if I was unhappy I could

128

leave. So instead of sitting back down and keeping quiet, I turned around and walked out the door assuming, although no one should ever assume anything as I learned later in life, that the other guys were right behind me. But they weren't. So I had a choice either to go back in, sit down, and behave myself or accept what success I had already had, be happy about it, and walk away. I thought I could live with that, but I knew I couldn't go back in there and hang my head down in shame. So I headed for the elevator and the only one who followed me out of that meeting was Lover Patterson. He followed me to the elevator and absolutely insisted that I stay in show business. And for a while there, that wasn't so easy. It got to the point that I couldn't even pay the rent on the little place I had with my wife. So Lover went and pawned all his clothes and all his jewelry and gave me the money to pay the rent. He had more faith in me than I had in myself. Lover was the guy that made me believe in me. He said he'd stick with me and I said, "I'll stick with you." The reason I'm here talking to you today is because of Lover Patterson.

Is he still alive?

Unfortunately, no, but he was here when I had other hits like "Spanish Harlem" and alive and well through all those recordings. He took the whole trip with us.

Was there anyone who influenced you musically whom you never got a chance to talk with?

So many. One of the ones I would have really liked to talk to was Billy Eckstine. He had all that class and style and sometimes I wish I had gone in that direction. He had that "gentleman" thing about him that I really enjoyed watching. I loved his voice; I really thought he was a great balladeer. Billy was one, but there were so, so many other great ones out there. Duke Ellington was another person I wish I had met, because of his talent, his dedication, and his love of music. Later on, I had a chance to talk to Sam Cooke. He taught me a lot and it was a privilege just watching him do what he did so well. So many great ones, but the first one that pops up in my head is Billy Eckstine.

Did anyone ever try to discourage you?

There was this woman in charge of the choir in my public school. This is when I was in PS 10 up in Harlem and I was thrown out of choir. She said, "You're too loud and have no voice control," or whatever and she put me out of the choir, which almost damaged me for life. Can't remember her name. Later on, I guess you could say that "loud voice" got me a couple of solos. Or maybe she was right.

Ben E. King, New York City, 1996

*Carole King on
"I Feel the Earth Move"*

I Feel the Earth Move

Words and Music by Carole King

I feel the earth move under my feet
I feel the sky tumbling down
I feel my heart start to trembling
Whenever you're around

Oh, baby, when I see your face
Mellow as the month of May
Oh, darling, I can't stand it
When you look at me that way

I feel the earth move under my feet
I feel the sky tumbling down
I feel my heart start to trembling
Whenever you're around

Instrumental

Oh, darling, when you're near me
And you tenderly call my name
I know that my emotions
Are something that I just can't tame
I've just got to have you baby

I feel the earth move under my feet
I feel the sky tumbling down, tumbling down
I feel the earth move under my feet
I feel the sky tumbling down, tumbling down

I just lose control
Down to my very soul
I get hot and cold all over

I feel the earth move under my feet
I feel the sky tumbling down
Tumbling down
Tumbling down
Tumbling down
Tumbling down

Chapter 17

Carole King

PHOTO: MICHAEL OCHS ARCHIVES.COM

I Feel The Earth Move

Chorus: I feel the earth move under my feet
           I feel the sky tumbling down
           I feel my heart start to trembling
           Whenever you're around

Oh, baby, when I see your face
Mellow as the month of May
Oh, darling, I can't stand it
When you look at me that way

Chorus

Instrumental

Oh, darling, when you're near me
And you tenderly call my name
I know that my emotions
Are something I just can't tame

I've just got to have you baby

I feel the earth move under my feet
I feel the sky tumbling down
I just lose control
Down to my very soul
I get hot and cold all over

I feel the earth move under my feet
I feel the sky tumbling down,
tumbling down
tumbling down
tumbling down
tumbling down
tumbling down

Carole King

"*Actually, this is one thing I have come to know about myself: Wherever my life journey carries me, and it often takes me far afield of my career, I always come home to songwriting. I am first, last, and always a songwriter.*"

"If people hear my songs and say, 'You know, that's exactly how I feel,' then I have been successful in making a connection."

Carole King

PHOTO: JIM McCRARY

"I Feel the Earth Move," written by Carole King, was recorded by Carole King for Ode Records in 1971. It was charted for fifteen weeks on Billboard's Hot 100 *and appeared on her Grammy Award–winning album,* Tapestry, *which remained on the album charts for 302 weeks. Inducted into the Songwriters Hall of Fame in 1987 and the Rock and Roll Hall of Fame in 1990, Carole King lives in Los Angeles, California.*

I was born in New York City on February 9, 1942, the same year—one week and an ocean apart—as Graham Nash. Growing up in New York City in the late forties and the early fifties, I was definitely exposed to a lot of cultural influences: classical music, theater, Broadway, and the earliest beginnings of rock and roll and rhythm and blues. It was truly a great time and place to be born. Sadly, I don't think anything like that kind of window of opportunity still exists now. It was before the "corporatization" of so many things, including the music business.

Was there much music in your family when you were growing up?

My parents loved and listened to music all the time. My mom had studied piano, so she was able to give me some rudimentary training, and there was always a piano in the house.

Do you draw inspiration from other creative arts and artists when you write?

I do draw inspiration, not only from other singers and songwriters, but also from films and books. One example is "I Feel the Earth Move," which I was inspired to write after finishing Hemingway's *For Whom the Bell Tolls,* in which making love was so beautifully and powerfully defined as "feeling the earth move." I think you can also find the breath of an early Motown influence in the way some of the background vocals come in ["I can't staaaaaand it"].

Do you tend to write a song out mostly in your head first or do you take the beginnings of an idea and then work it out at the piano?

It varies from song to song. Some songs start with a lyrical idea and some with a musical idea, but all songs start with an idea. Ideas and inspiration can come from just about anywhere. When you're writing on assignment, like for a film, the inspiration often simply comes from the project. When you're writing for an artist, you'll often write from your knowledge or feeling of that artist. And then other times, it just comes from nowhere that you can name—it's just there, and you don't question it.

Did being a woman ever present itself as a difficulty or an obstacle in attaining success in this business?

I never had anybody who tried to stop me from doing what I was doing. In fact, it has in more recent years been brought to my attention that being a woman in this male-dominated business might have stopped me, but it didn't. Women today continue to tell me they're grateful to me for breaking that barrier. I just never saw the barrier. Obviously, there was one, but it never made itself known to me. I just went ahead thinking that I had as good a shot of accomplishing what I wanted to accomplish as anybody, male or female. I'd suppose that's apparently what did break the barrier—the fact that I didn't see it as a "barrier." So maybe the lesson is that if you don't really see the problem, then in a way, it isn't there.

Can you remember the first time that you heard something you had written on the radio?

You know, I can't remember a specific year, but the one moment I remember the most was sitting in a car with Gerry Goffin, who was then my husband and co-writer, and hearing, "Will You Love Me Tomorrow?" on the radio for the first time. It was an unbelievable feeling. To this day, when I hear something I've done that I really care about or that I've invested a lot of time or energy in, such as my album *Love Makes the World*, I still feel that same kind of, "Oh my God, it's out there!" excitement.

Does your being able to communicate with so many people through your music ever cross your mind when you're writing?

Generally, I do my "talking" outside my work. My work is about writing a really good song that will move people. Sometimes the song may have some political implications with a message, but generally for me, it's all about writing a really good pop song. A pop song deals mainly with emotions, so if my mission is to write a real song, then of course, my goal is to deal with emotions.

When you made your new album, Love Makes the World, *did your approach vary in any significant way from other albums you've recorded in the past?*

PHOTO: JIM McCRARY

There are always things about the process that are the same, as well as things that are different, with each project. I'm almost always writing songs, and eventually, at the right time, a certain group of songs simply speaks out as the right collection for a Carole King album. With *Love Makes the World*, for example, I had the luxury of time. I collaborated with a variety of different songwriters over a period of three or four years and had the time to really craft and select the songs for it, and then record them with the kind of quality I wanted for this album.

Why do you think Tapestry *struck such a deep and resonant chord within so many people?*

I really have no idea. In the making of it, there was no conscious effort to meet any particular need. I just selected songs that felt were right and recorded them simply, and at that particular time it seemed to be what people wanted to hear. I am very happy that *Tapestry* continues to reach and touch people. That time was a very artistic and special time.

What do you think it is about your songs that make them have such lasting resonance?

PHOTO: MICHAEL OCHS ARCHIVES.COM

I don't know, I guess I just write what I feel or what I observe in life. It's important to me to keep it simple and true. If people hear my songs and say "You know, that's exactly how I feel," then I have been successful in making a connection. I feel so lucky to be able to make that connection with my work.

Do you think there is a lack of melody in songwriting today?

I've been asked this before and I don't think that is particularly true. There are many songs today that make good use of melody; it's just that it might be harder to find them. There is so much product out there now that is competing to be heard in a field where equal opportunity doesn't necessarily apply. So often it turns out that the product with the most money behind it is what gets heard. No, melodic music did not go away—we just have to look beyond what is being placed in front of us to find it.

You seem to have made a very conscious effort to avoid becoming a prisoner of your own celebrity, while there are other artists who don't seem to have been as lucky.

Yes, I know a lot of those people. I consciously didn't ever want that to happen to me because an important part of my life is being able to live life just as anyone else would. I realize I'm better off than most and without question, I have a certain amount of freedom because of that, but I love my work and I love my life. It's had its ups and downs, but it's all part of living. My primary directive is to put life first and then my career as it fits into that life. If I didn't, I'd lose touch with myself. And if I'm being in touch with myself, then I'm in touch with others, because I believe we're all interconnected. Our commonality is something that is incredibly important to both me and my work. In general, what's important to me is to maintain a love of learning and to see if it's possible to leave the world a better place than I found it.

When you sit down to write, is there anything that can tear you away from the piano?

Raising four kids, and the word "Mom" coming from another room.

Have you ever envisioned a time when you wouldn't be writing songs?

I've been writing songs since I was very young, I think in the single digits. Gerry and I wrote our very first hit song "Will You Love Me Tomorrow?" when I was seventeen. Actually, this is one thing I have come to know about myself: Wherever my life journey carries me, and it often takes me far afield of my career, I always come home to songwriting. I am first, last, and always a songwriter.

Do you have any advice for aspiring songwriters?

My advice is to be true to who you are. Just be yourself. Don't try and be what other people tell you that you ought to be, and don't give up. More than anything else, you just have to persevere. There was a young woman, whose name I'm not going to mention, who was terribly afraid that her record company was going to find out she was thirty-three years old. Thirty-three! And this was all because the record industry, and I'm talking about the "industry" part of it, has the kind of corporate executives who continue to make these kind of decisions, and in doing so, can be cruelly ageist. Crowding sixty [years of age], and with a new album, I knew I was going to have to face that

"industry" attitude. So I decided I'd release the album myself and do it without them because in my case, my audience doesn't care how old I am; they just care if I write good songs and the music they like. I was trying to tell this girl the same thing. I was horrified that she, at thirty-three, felt that she was going to be discriminated against because of her age. It's bad enough when you play twelve really good songs you've written for a record company and then they turn around and tell you, "I don't hear a hit single." In those cases, no one is ever going to get to hear those twelve good songs and it's all just because someone didn't hear a "hit single."

I'm very well aware of commercial reality. If you as an artist are always chasing commercial reality, then you're killing the very thing that makes you unique and special. But to be fair, I suppose I have to say that I got my own start as a songwriter writing for a "commercial" reality. And we also put a lot of art and heart into doing that. But it was much easier back in those days to get something that was different heard. These days, if you're not the next Britney [Spears] or 'N Sync, or if you're not operating on the current formula they can identify with, then the corporate executives won't really give you a shot. I'm really happy that I've been able to start my own record label and put my music out on my own and get right to the people. It's been great. The sales may not be what they could have been if someone at the top of the heap at a big label was behind them, but I also know that every person who's buying my album is doing so not because it was thrown in their face eighty times a day, but

PHOTO: JIM McCRARY

because they wanted to find it. If you aren't true to yourself, then you're just imitating what's already been done. You may be able to do that very well and make a living, but you're certainly not feeding your soul, which is what is unique to you.

Has being a performer and being able to communicate directly to an audience been as meaningful an experience as songwriting itself?

There's not any one thing I'm really proud of. There are a lot of things in my life that I don't go public about. I love my life, I love what I'm doing, and I love that I've been able to achieve the success that I have, and that's been amazing. I also love that I've been able to have the freedom to make choices. One of the reasons I don't tour is because, for me, when you're locked into a schedule for "x" amount of time, then you have to be in a certain place and on stage every night. I can't do that. I like performing. When I'm doing a show, it's something very special for me and I'm there for a particular purpose as opposed to merely showing up because it's one of fifty dates scheduled on a tour. That's not to either put down or denigrate anybody who goes on tour. For example, I know Crosby, Stills, Nash & Young love those two hours every night. They can't wait to get on the stage, and God bless them because we're all the richer for it. But for me, my choice is to try and make each thing I do in my life special, whether it's a performance, or writing a song, my environmental lobbying work, or whatever. I do it because it's meaningful to me. So I'd have to say I'm proud of all of the above.

Disc Two
Track 6

Graham Nash on
"Our House"

Our House
Graham Nash

I'll light the fire
You place the flowers in the vase
That you bought today.
Staring at the fire
For hours and hours while I listen
To you play your love songs
All night long for me, only for me.

Come to me now,
And rest your head for just five minutes,
Everything is done.
Such a cozy room
The windows are illuminated by the
Evening sunshine through them
Fiery gems for you, only for you.

Our house is a very, very, very fine house.
With two cats in the yard,
Life used to be so hard,
Now everything is easy 'cause of you.

I'll light the fire
While you place the flowers in the vase
That you bought today.

Chapter 18

Graham Nash

PHOTO: TIM OWEN

Our House

I'll light the fire
you place the flowers in the vase
that you bought today —
Staring at the fire
for hours and hours while I listen
to you play your love songs
all night long for me - only for me

Come to me now
and rest your head for just five minutes
Everything is done
Such a cosy room
the windows are illuminated by the
evening sunshine through them
Fiery gems for me - only for me

Our house is a very, very, very fine house
with two cats in the yard
life used to be so hard
Now everything is easy 'cos of you
and Our House

"I was crossing the floor and 'Bye Bye Love' by the Everly Brothers came on and it just stopped both of us cold. We'd never heard anything like it before. To this day I've always tried to make music that does for others what 'Bye Bye Love' did for me then."

PHOTO: ©HENRY DILTZ/
CHANSLEY ENTERTAINMENT ARCHIVES

"When I was just thirteen, I spent my time in school practicing my autograph instead of doing math. I'd be drawing stage setups, amps, drums, where I'd put the speakers and the Fender guitars."

Crosby, Stills, Nash & Young

PHOTO: ©HENRY DILTZ/
CHANSLEY ENTERTAINMENT ARCHIVES

"Our House," written by Graham Nash, was recorded by Crosby, Stills, Nash & Young for Atlantic Records in 1970. It climbed the music charts for six weeks and peaked at #30 on Billboard's Hot 100. *Graham Nash, cofounder of the Hollies in 1962, had a string of top forty hits with the group; most notably "Bus Stop" and "Carrie Anne." After moving to the United States, he co-founded the folk/rock group Crosby, Stills & Nash in 1968. Crosby, Stills & Nash were inducted into the Rock and Roll Hall of Fame in 1997. Graham Nash lives in Los Angeles, California.*

I was born in Blackpool, in the north of England, on February 2, 1942, at 1:15 A.M. The reason I was born in Blackpool, which is not where we lived, was that during the closing years of the Second World War, pregnant women were evacuated from bombing areas to have their babies in peace. Blackpool is about fifty miles from Salford, which is a suburb of Manchester, where we actually lived. Blackpool is basically the Coney Island of England; it's got the fun fair on the beach and all those seaside kind of things. It wasn't a strategic or primary target for the German bombers like Manchester. So even though we lived in Salford, I was born in Blackpool.

Would you say that songwriting is mainly a matter of inspiration?

I would have to say that it's something you can't do unless you are inspired, so inspiration has to be at least 75 percent of the equation.

What form does that inspiration come in?

With music, it's usually an incident that happens to me—something personal, something I've read in the paper or witnessed on the street, even something someone has said.

PHOTO: ©EBET ROBERTS/
CHANSLEY ENTERTAINMENT ARCHIVES

If you were going to be your toughest critic, what would you say are your strengths and weaknesses as a writer?

My weak point is that I never learned the language of music. I don't read music and I don't know that many who do among my peers. I know Neil [Young] doesn't, I know Stephen [Stills] doesn't, David [Crosby] doesn't, and I'm not sure if Joni [Mitchell] does. So one of my weaknesses is that I don't know the language, but at this stage of the game, I'm not sure it matters. If I have a strength it may be that I have learned to be accepting of these gifts from wherever it is that they come.

It must have been an adjustment leaving England, where the Hollies were very popular, for the relative obscurity of the United States.

The first time that I came to this country was in 1965 with the Hollies. We came to New York and played a show at the Paramount Theater. It was *The Soupy Sales Easter Extravaganza*. We were one of maybe twenty acts and each act did two songs. We thought we were coming to America to do "shows." The stage manager said, "Okay, what two songs are you gonna do?" And we said, "Two songs, what are you talking about?" Each of these twenty acts all did two songs, five shows a day, starting at ten-thirty in the morning and that was a different concept for us. America was this fascinating, wonderful, eye-opening, ever-embracing heaven for me. In England, if you didn't know John and Paul and George and Ringo,

David Crosby, Stephen Stills & Graham Nash, 1969

PHOTO COURTESY OF SHOWTIME
MUSIC ARCHIVES(TORONTO)

you really weren't anybody. At least that's how it appeared to me. There used to be an imaginary line just south of Birmingham, which is in the Midlands. It was as if everybody who lived and died above that line were peasants, and the farther north you got, the more "peasanty" you were and the less people took notice of what you thought. Then the Beatles came along and blew that whole thing wide open. Before that, if you wanted to be taken seriously you spoke the "Queen's English." But all of a sudden, people were trying to fake Liverpool accents and then it all started to really change. It was so different in America. Here people wanted to know what I thought, people wanted to know my opinion. I was in a different world, and I didn't want to go back to England.

Was it in the United States or in England that you first felt you had some real success?

It was definitely there. You've got to understand the way it was in England. The normal process was that you did what your dad did, and you did what his dad did before him. "If it was good enough for him, then it's good enough for you, son!" My mother and father never instilled that in me. Early on, my mother and father saw I had a real passion for music. When I was just thirteen, I spent my time in school practicing my autograph instead of doing math. I'd be drawing stage setups, amps, drums, where I'd put the speakers and the Fender guitars. All I wanted to do was play music, and from a very early age my mother and father supported that passion. Later in life, I asked my mother why she had done that and she said she'd always wanted to go on the stage. She'd envisioned a life in show business for herself but during World War II she had married my father and had three kids, so it wasn't feasible for her. So in a way, it turned out she was vicariously living her life through me. It's all very interesting.

Was there anyone you especially wanted to succeed for?

His name was Ron Richards. He was the man who came to the Cavern for a lunchtime show in Liverpool and saw the Hollies play. He saw me playing my guitar without strings because the night before, I'd busted my last one and couldn't afford new ones. He thought that was very cheeky and very cool. He saw the show and then asked us to come and record. Ron had a faith and a vision for the Hollies that was extremely important to us at that time in our careers. Somebody believed in us, other than us. He supported us, guided us, and taught us how to record and what hit records were meant to sound like. I always tried to

PHOTO: ©HENRY DILTZ/
CHANSLEY ENTERTAINMENT ARCHIVES

do my best for Ron Richards. He was very influential at a time in my life that I needed a mentor and a guide and he was that man. I would have done anything for Ron.

Did anyone ever try and stand in the way of your career?

There was a man named Mr. Lewis and I think he was my geography teacher at school. By doing something vicious to me, he also made my life better. It goes like this. One day in 1958, Bill Haley came to play the Palace Theater in Manchester. I took a day off to go and stand in line and get a ticket. Somehow, Mr. Lewis saw me in that line. So my excuse that I was too sick to go to school just got me sent straight to the headmaster's office instead, where I was given a severe punishment for taking the day off and for lying about it.

Severely punished?

The six strokes with "the slipper" across my ass weren't very pleasant. But they certainly helped me justify my lying and taking the day off by making me think if someone was not

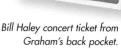

going to recognize my passion and instead would punish me for just wanting to improve my life, then that can't be right. You must understand, I thought of rock and roll as improving my life while a lot of parents and teachers thought that rock and roll was ruining our lives. You're not going to believe this unless I show you, but to this day, in my back pocket, I still have my Bill Haley ticket. I've carried it for over forty years. This ticket changed my life. You think that was important to me? Do you know how many things I've had in my life that have been misplaced or lost? That ticket's been with me every day. Two shillings, that's just over a quarter. I sat in the balcony and it absolutely changed my life.

Bill Haley concert ticket from Graham's back pocket.

Was music important to you when you were a kid?

When I was a kid living in Salford, we only had the one radio and on it you had four stations, all controlled by the BBC. There was this one station, Radio Luxemburg, that played the American top forty on Sunday night at about nine o'clock. Now at nine P.M. on a Sunday night, I'm supposed to be in bed for school the next day but somehow I managed to persuade my parents to listen to the top forty on the radio in the kitchen, which was one floor below my bedroom. I also had figured out that the bedpost conducted the sound of the radio from the kitchen below. And that's how I heard the American top forty, with my ear pressed to the bedpost.

What were some of the songs you were listening to?

"Bye Bye Love" changed my life. One evening, I went to this Saturday night dance with my friend Allan Clarke. We went down these stairs, handed our tickets to the girl, went through a door and a record called "You Send Me" by Sam Cooke had just ended and everybody was walking off the dance floor because of the break in the music. I was crossing the floor and "Bye Bye Love" by the Everly Brothers came on and it just stopped both of us cold. We'd never heard anything like it before. To this day I've always tried to make music that does for others what "Bye Bye Love" did for me then.

You're also known for your great passion for photography. Did your family play a role in that when you were growing up?

My father was an amateur photographer and he bought a camera from a friend of his at work. We'd put up a blanket against the window in my room to block out the light and we'd develop and print the film with this primitive setup with an enlarger and stuff. My dad was the one who turned me on to photography. He'd put the blank paper into this colorless liquid and say, "Wait now, patience, patience," and then thirty seconds later this image of me on an elephant or something would just appear out of nothing. It was magic to me, and I've never lost that sense of magic. Then one day the police came to the door. They said the camera my father had bought had originally been stolen, and they wanted to know whom it was that had sold it to him. My father refused to tell them. Long story short, for a thirty-dollar camera they put him in jail for a year, and it broke his heart. That was in 1953. I became the man of the family. I was eleven.

Did you ever go to see your dad when he was there?

I never went to see him, no. He didn't want me to. It destroyed him and it destroyed his life.

Did he live to see you have some success?

With the Hollies, yes, there were two, three years of early success. He was a really proud man. I mean, one of his kids had made it out of that hellhole and made it to London. His greatest dream was to go to Wembley Stadium to see the Cup final, but he never made it. Wembley Stadium was only 182 miles away, and he never made it. So the first thing I did when CSN&Y [Crosby, Stills, Nash & Young] played Wembley Stadium, and we filled the place, was that I went on the field and kicked a ball about for my dad. He would have been very pleased.

Do you have any advice for a young aspiring songwriter?

Absolutely. You have to love what you're doing and you have to search your heart and write from that place. And it's my observation, for what it's worth, that profoundly moving sounds usually spring from a great truth.

Crosby, Stills & Nash Tour
Saratoga Performing Arts Center
Saratoga Springs, New York, August 25, 2001

PHOTO: BUZZ PERSON

Crosby, Stills & Nash
2001 Tour playlist

You're a man of many interests. At this point in your life, how are your creative energies divided?

They're not divided at all; my great love is being able to create, period. No matter which way I turn, whether it's making a piece of sculpture, creating a new song, or uncovering some treasure in a dusty attic somewhere, whether it's trying to be the best husband and the best father I can be to my kids, I'm just incredibly grateful that I can create. I don't know what it is, I don't know how it happens, and I don't question it. I've been an unbelievably lucky man all my life, and it seems to me that my mother was right when she told me, "Just go out into the world; no harm will come to you if you lead with your heart." And that's all I've ever done. It seems to have stood me in good stead. I'm still here, I'm sixty years old, and I'm still rocking my ass off.

PHOTO: TONY BITTICK

145

John Sebastian on
"Do You Believe in Magic"

Do You Believe in Magic

John Sebastian

Do You Believe in Magic in a young girl's heart?
How the music can free her whenever it starts.
And it's magic if the music is groovy
And makes you feel happy like an old-time movie.
I'll tell you about the magic and it can free your soul
But it's like tryin' to tell a stranger 'bout a rock and roll.

If you believe in magic don't you bother to choose,
If it's jug band music or rhythm and blues.
Just go and listen, it'll start with a smile
That won't wipe off your face no matter how hard you try.
Your feet start tappin' and you can't seem to find
How you got there—so just blow your mind.

If you believe in magic come along with me.
We'll dance until morning till there's just you and me
And maybe if the music is right
I'll meet you tomorrow sorta late at night.
And we'll go dancin' baby, then you'll see
How the magic's in the music and the music's in me. Yeah!

Do you believe like I believe?
Do you believe like I believe? Yeah!

Believe in the magic of a young girl's soul
Believe in the magic of rock and roll
Believe in the magic that can set you free
Ohh, talking 'bout magic

Chapter 19

John Sebastian

PHOTO: ©HENRY DILTZ/
CHANSLEY ENTERTAINMENT ARCHIVES

Do You Believe in Magic

Do you believe in magic in a young girl's heart
How the music can free her whenever it starts
and it's magic if the music is groovy
and makes you feel happy like an old time movie
I'll tell you 'bout the magic – it can free your soul
But it's like tryin' to tell a stranger 'bout rock & roll

If you believe in magic – don't bother to choose
If it's jug band music or rythm and blues
Just go and listen… It'll start with a smile
That won't wipe off your face no matter how hard
you try
Your feet start tappin' and you can't seem to find
How you got there – so just blow your mind

If you believe in magic – come along with me
We'll dance until morning 'till there's just you and me
and maybe if the music is right
I'll meet you tomorrow sort of late at night
and we'll go dancin, baby, then you'll see
How the magic's in the music and the
music's in me – Yeah!
Do you believe in magic?
Believe in the magic of a young girl's soul
Believe in the magic of rock & roll
Believe in the magic that can set you free

Do you believe like I believe
Do you believe like I believe
Do you believe like I believe
    repeat with vocal ad lib and fade

John Sebastian

148

"I remember playing in the
basement of Gerde's Folk City.
Bob Dylan and I always
seemed to be playing there at
the same time. He'd open for
Victoria Spivey, this wonderful
old blues singer who'd sponsored
a little jug band that I had
gotten myself into."

"We'd play in these basket houses, like Charlie Washburn's Third Side, and then pass the hat. If you were lucky, you got the hat back."

The Lovin' Spoonful

"Do You Believe in Magic," written by John Sebastian, was recorded by the Lovin' Spoonful for Kama Sutra Records in 1965. Released as the group's first single, it climbed the charts for eight weeks and then hit #9 on Billboard's Hot 100. It has since reached over three million broadcast performances as certified by BMI. In 2000, the Lovin' Spoonful was inducted into the Rock and Roll Hall of Fame. John Sebastian currently resides in Woodstock, New York.

I was born in New York City on Saint Paddy's Day in 1944. I was so lucky to be born and raised in the city at that time and growing up in Greenwich Village. Just being sixteen in 1960 was lucky. Being able to see the parade of great guitarists, blues singers, bluegrass guys, and even scary Appalachian ladies like Jean Ritchie, I mean, how could the wonderful intersection of all that music not have an effect on you? You probably could have gotten more of Mississippi by growing up in Mississippi, but if you couldn't grow up there, you were going to get more of Mississippi by being in Greenwich Village than anywhere else at that time.

Do you think songwriting is mainly inspiration?

Different songs have different proportions of inspiration and perspiration. "Hitdom" is not always the indicator of how much work went into the song. Lots of very valuable copyrights fell out of the sky in three minutes. On the other hand, I've taken a whole summer to refine a four or five-minute song. One of the songs I'm thinking of is a tune called "A Face of Appalachia," which by no means was a hit song. It all started with a tape Lowell George and I were sending back and forth to each other and it took the whole summer tinkering with it to get it right. But that's just the musical trench-digging type of work that can go on sometimes.

At The Farm, an artistic community in Lake Hollywood, California, 1969

Did you start out playing in clubs?

The whole music scene in New York really didn't start out in clubs; it started in Washington Square at Sunday afternoon get-togethers. That's where all of us were trying out our very first Lightnin' Hopkins guitar licks or our bluegrass G runs. It included guys like David Grisman, myself, and Richie Havens, who at the time was a doo-wop singer making food money by working as a painter, a sketch artist who does caricatures of people on the street. From giving it away in Washington Square on Sundays, we went to working in basket houses, which were unlicensed clubs that mostly didn't have liquor licenses. They sold really bad versions of espresso, which was really just two scoops of Sanka, salt, and cinnamon. We'd play in these basket houses, like Charlie Washburn's Third Side, and then pass the hat. If you were lucky, you got the hat back. I remember playing in the basement of Gerde's Folk City. Bob Dylan and I always seemed to be playing there at the same time. He'd open for Victoria Spivey, this wonderful old blues singer who'd sponsored a little jug band that I had gotten myself into. All this was a really great foundation, a wonderful practice session for what was to come. Maria Muldaur always laughs about this

because we were just incredibly lucky little New York shits to have played Town Hall and Carnegie Hall all within the same six months. Playing Carnegie Hall and I was just seventeen years old! I remember calling up my dad to say, "Hey, Dad, my jug band finally got an actual gig." And he said, "Oh, great, where are you playing?" I answered, "Well, it's Carnegie Hall." You have to understand, my father was a classical musician who had spent time touring the South back in those days, trying to get some respect for this unorthodox instrument he was playing. He played the classical repertoire on the harmonica, so in some ways, he was already a kind of underdog. Traveling around the South he'd hear Sonny Boy Williamson and Sonny Terry, guys like that. When I was around sixteen, I went to the taping of a television show where Sam [Samuel Sebastian] was playing. I remember Lightnin' Hopkins was on the bill with an unknown Joan Baez. Sam was perfectly comfortable with their music and considered each of them serious musicians. I was lucky enough to be there just to absorb that confluence of those good energies. I really benefited from that.

PHOTO: ©HENRY DILTZ/CHANSLEY ENTERTAINMENT ARCHIVES

So music wasn't just an ambition for you; it was almost genetic.

Absolutely. When I was still in my mid-teens, I remember playing a sleazy club called Café Bizarre. The good thing about the Café Bizarre was that it had no local audience. Nobody from Greenwich Village would have been caught dead in this place. But what the owner of the Bizarre did was to import busloads of tourists, who'd come in to see the "beatniks." That was the draw for the out-of-towners, "See Greenwich Village. Stop in to a real beatnik coffeehouse." The upside for the Spoonful was that we weren't playing just for the Greenwich Village-ites. It was probably also the best thing that could have happened to us at that point because we were snotty Village kids who thought we knew everything. So it was really good to go and play for folks from Dayton, Ohio, and find out what really held their attention, find out what played in the larger world outside the Village.

Was your songwriting affected at all by those early days of playing for such diverse audiences?

I think in some sense it's true. I never wanted the music to be dark like Nico was in the sixties or anything. We were just a couple of years too old for that sort of dark scene and, besides, it was going to be too much like "Yeah, yeah, and you can't play either, so get out of here with all that depressing shit."

Do you feel like you have to chase the muse?

Different periods of my life have dictated different patterns. When I'm asked, "What comes first, the music or the lyrics?," a famous songwriter, whose name escapes me for the moment, answered, "What comes first? The phone call." And I thought that's really on the money because as a songwriter, like it or not, you're often faced with a demand for material. Sometimes the phone call can be the bank manager telling you you're overdrawn. That's a very solid stimulus.

John Sebastian, 1996

PHOTO: ©EBET ROBERTS/
CHANSLEY ENTERTAINMENT ARCHIVES

When you need a distraction, what do you turn to?

Guitars and the mechanics of guitars and how they go together. Trying to keep them clean and ready for action provides a kind of distraction for me. I've always had a little guitar bench that I often go to when the songwriting isn't going well. I work on an instrument hoping it will give up the goods a little easier. It's sort of like, each time I wash the car it seems to run better. It just seems to know.

Did you ever have any unusual events happen during collaborations that ended up in the finished work?

All the time. There was a musical fragment that Steve Boone used to play at our rehearsals whenever there was a keyboard available. It was just a circular thing that didn't seem to go anywhere. But he would just play this thing and it became a joke at the Spoonful rehearsals. I'd constantly find myself saying, "Steve, that's neither a verse nor is it a chorus. Please, let's play something else." Then one day we found ourselves in the process of writing "Summer in the City." The verse and the chorus were together but we found ourselves looking for a middle theme. Just then, Steve plays that annoying "Bum, pada, dom-dom, bad-om, bum-bum" thing and I said, "That's the best middle eight this song could ever have." It suddenly evoked this image of traffic and a bustling city, even before we started fiddling with the idea of adding car horns. You know that movement in Gershwin's "An American in Paris"? That was very much on our minds when that middle eight suddenly found its home. It was just a happy accident.

When was the first time you realized your music had gained acceptance?

Well, there was this one particular night we were playing the Night Owl Café owned by the infamous Joe Marra. He's an amazing, crazy fuckin' guy who couldn't fuckin' say two fuckin' sentences together without saying "fuckin'"—one of those true New York kind of guys. And to this day, I still exchange Christmas cards with him. Anyway, we were playing pretty steadily for the local people from Greenwich Village who were part of the jazz scene or part of the kind of downtown "in crowd." They were "finger poppers," guys who played chess, "beatniks." But one night as we were playing, I looked out in the audience and saw this beautiful little sixteen-year-old girl just dancing the night away. And I remember Zally [Zalman Yanovsky] and I just elbowed each other the entire night because to us that young girl symbolized the fact that our audience was changing, that maybe they had finally found us. I wrote "Do You Believe in Magic" the next day.

Was there anyone who influenced you musically whom you wished you had met?

Well I never got to meet Elvis and he was absolutely an early influence in my work. I guess talking to him would have been a pretty big thing. I first heard "Heartbreak Hotel" when I was twelve and living in Italy. It was playing on the Armed Forces Radio Network and I was blown away. But the only information I could get was that the guy was born in Tupelo, Mississippi, and smoked marijuana. Funny thing, by the time I got back to the States there was no more talk of the marijuana. I don't know, maybe that was AFR's [Armed Forces Radio]

John Sebastian onstage at Woodstock, 1969

PHOTO: ©HENRY DILTZ/ CHANSLEY ENTERTAINMENT ARCHIVES

way of explaining how this guy was able to get this "loose thing" going. But if I had ever met the "King," I would have told him, "Fuck all those guys at RCA. Get back to the Sun [Records] thing." It's unfortunate he got so ensnared in so much third-rate material. I mean, Leiber and Stoller writing songs for you is one thing; they were writing great songs, they really understood this media. It's all that other shit that killed him.

Was there someone you especially wanted to succeed for or prove yourself to?

John in the studio with his father

PHOTO: DON PAULSON

Yes. And as an incredible bonus, a young photographer just happened to catch the moment in a photograph I value maybe above all others. Like I've said, my dad was a classical musician; my mother was also a writer and wrote very funny stuff for the radio. But neither of them were overly impressed by our first flushes of success because they knew quick, fleeting fame wouldn't mean being able to put food on the table next year. I think we were into our second album when I got asked to do the sound track for the film _You're a Big Boy Now_. And there I was in the studio in front of a full orchestra playing harmonica, and my dad walked in. I think that moment symbolized the first time he knew we were going to have some kind of a viable career and, for me, that was tremendously gratifying.

153

Grace Slick on
"White Rabbit"

White Rabbit

Grace Slick

One pill makes you larger
And one pill makes you small.
And the one that mother gives you
Don't do anything at all.
Go ask Alice
When she's ten feet tall.

And if you go chasing rabbits
And you know you're going to fall.
Tell 'em a hookah smoking caterpillar
Has given you the call.
He called Alice
When she was just small.

When the men on the chessboard
Get up and tell you where to go.
And you've just had some kind of mushroom
And your head is moving slow
Go ask Alice
I think she'll know.

When logic and proportion
Have fallen sloppy dead
And the White Knight is talking backwards
And the Red Queen is off with her head
Remember what the Dormouse said
Feed your head, feed your head.

Chapter 20

Grace Slick

PHOTO: ©JIM STEINFELDT/
CHANSLEY ENTERTAINMENT ARCHIVES

White Rabbit

The pill makes you larger
and one pill makes you small
and the ones that mother gives you
don't do anything at all

Go ask Alice when she's ten feet tall

If you go chasing rabbits
and you know your going to fall
Tell 'em a hookah smoking caterpillar
has given you the call
He called Alice when she was just small
when the men on the chessboard
Get up and tell you where to go
and you've just had some kind of mushroom
and your mind is moving low

Go ask Alice I think she'll know

when logic and proportion
have fallen sloppy dead
and the white knights talking backwords
and the Red Queens off with her head

Remember what the doormouse said

FEED YOUR HEAD !

Grace Slick

"Then I went to see Jefferson Airplane playing at the Matrix in San Francisco and I thought, 'Boy, that job looks a lot better than the one I have. They drink, smoke pot, and in one night, for maybe two and a half hours' work, they earn more than I do in a week.' . . . Besides, it's rock and roll, so how well do you really have to sing?"

"A good friend of mine once said to me, 'How do you live in that head? It's going all the time.' My answer was, 'I guess I'm just used to it.'"

Jefferson Airplane

PHOTO: MICHAEL OCHS ARCHIVES.COM

"White Rabbit," written by Grace Slick, was recorded by Jefferson Airplane for RCA Records in 1967. It enjoyed nine weeks on Billboard's Hot 100 *where it reached the #8 spot.* Surrealistic Pillow, *the album that included "White Rabbit," stayed on the charts for fifty-eight weeks and peaked at #3. Both "White Rabbit" (in 1998) and* Surrealistic Pillow *(in 1999) were inducted into the Grammy Hall of Fame. Grace Slick, along with the other members of Jefferson Airplane, was inducted into the Rock and Roll Hall of Fame in 1996. Grace Slick currently lives in Los Angeles, California.*

I was born in Highland Park or Evanston, Illinois; it's a little unclear. Anyway, it was in the suburbs of Chicago in 1939. When I was very young, my father's company transferred him to the West Coast, so L.A. is really the first town I can remember. After a year and a half in L.A. he was transferred again, this time to San Francisco. For a while we lived pretty much on Market Street, which is the main drag in San Francisco. Then I think my parents wanted a place where I could run around, play, and ride bicycles. So, we picked up and moved to Palo Alto, the home of Stanford University. Several really strange people like Pig Pen and Jerry Garcia and me came out of that very *Leave It to Beaver* community; I don't know why it spawned so many strange fish. Later, I pretty much exclusively lived in the Bay area. I'd get a new apartment or house or whatever about every six months, and I'd decorate them all differently. It was like living on a movie set. When I got tired of my surroundings, I'd move from set to set just for the hell of it. I couldn't move too far from San Francisco because of the band. But I'm just a born gypsy; if I can't move my house I'll kind of shift around in the place where I am, from room to room.

Is songwriting for you mainly based on inspiration or perspiration?

The perspiration comes after the inspiration. In other words, you get an idea either musically or lyrically. It may just be one line, but then you sit and think about that one line. Why does that one line affect me that way and how can I work it into the context of a song?

Jefferson Airplane, Los Angeles, 1967

PHOTO COURTESY OF SHOWTIME MUSIC ARCHIVES (TORONTO)/RANDY SHARRAD

Do you have to look for inspiration or does it just come to you?

I've never really had to chase it per se. Right now I have papers and papers with one-liners, half a song, a hook, or the middle verses written down on them. I have ideas written on file cards, and that pile is so high that I probably couldn't get it done in this lifetime. I don't have a problem with coming up with ideas. A good friend of mine said to me once, "How do you live in that head? It's going all the time." My answer was, "I guess I'm just used to it."

Do you have a special routine or place that gets you in a creative mood?

If I'm out in the car, I'll just pull over to the shoulder and write my ideas down on a file card. I've always done it with music and I do that with drawing. I have to write it down, because I have a good twenty-four-hour memory but from then on it's gone.

Do you think that where and when you grew up had an influence on your music?

They say that everything you've ever seen or heard or experienced is all registered in this gigantic computer that we have as a brain. In other words, you'll be walking around doing whatever you're doing and all of a sudden you'll remember something, and for no particular reason some memory will squirt through all those brain chemicals and present itself to your consciousness. Sometimes it's good and sometimes it isn't.

Was there someone along the way you wanted to succeed for?

I don't think so. I was never trying to prove anything. Before I got involved with the Airplane I wasn't even a so-called "serious musician." The fact is, I was a floor model for I. Magnin in San Francisco, which involved a lot of walking around the couturier department and wearing a different outfit every ten minutes. You're on your feet all day and obviously you can't take drugs. Then I went to see Jefferson Airplane playing at the Matrix in San Francisco and I thought, "Boy, that job looks a lot better than the one I have. They drink, smoke pot, and in one night, for maybe two and a half hours' work, they earn more than I do in a week." So I thought, "Okay, my mother was a singer for a while; I know what that is. I can do that." Besides, it's rock and roll, so how well do you really have to sing?

So this wasn't something you had always imagined doing?

Never. I hadn't even thought of it before I went to see them. But I knew I was going to be in the arts in one way or the other. Math, machinery, all that stuff is definitely not my thing. I don't even allow anybody to use the TV remote control in my house when they're over because they might press the wrong button and I'd have no idea how to get it back to where I had it set before. I'd have to call a TV guy to come over and fix it. So I knew between the arts and the sciences, it was definitely going to be the arts.

Given that, did you feel you had something to prove to yourself?

Just in the sense that you're always trying to do your best. Whether it's a song, or a painting, or a book, or whatever, it always needs to be made clear to the person you're communicating with, whether it's one person or a million. I'm constantly trying to be as clear as possible. But there's no set standard for singing over a hundred and thirty decibels of electric guitar. I was born for rock and roll, my voice is very loud, and it was relatively easy to do. But writing lyrics and constructing the songs, being in the studio, that's the part I find the most interesting.

What comes first for you when you're writing, the music or the lyrics?

At times the lyrics can come first; sometimes it's the music. It comes in all directions and forms. I can hear three notes or chords on television or on the radio anywhere and I think, oh, if that only ended with an A minor. Most creativity is theft anyway; everybody steals. You steal even when you don't know you're doing it.

When was it you first realized you had gained some degree of success?

I knew things had started to change when kids started coming up to us after the concerts and treating us like we were celebrities rather than just the regular assholes we knew we were. I also knew things had changed when RCA paid for us to stay in a big house in L.A. for six months where the Beatles used to stay. I don't know what it cost to put us up in that house, but I thought RCA must probably be doing well from us if they were willing to do that.

How did you feel about hearing your music on the radio for the first time?

It was weird then and it's even weirder now. I find it funny that anyone would still be interested in listening to it. At a gallery opening a while back, I was showing my paintings and some guy came up to me and said, "You know, I used to work in the Clinton White House and they played your music a lot." Weird, huh? Even twenty years ago, somebody once wrote to me and said there was a university professor teaching a course on the Airplane's lyrics. I thought that was so funny because I don't think of myself as anyone to study or teach about. Basically, we just hoped someone might buy an album, go home, listen to it, and be thinking the music's not bad and those lyrics about James Joyce, or whatever it is she's singing, yada-yada-yada, maybe they might be amused. That was all we ever hoped for.

Do you have the same attitude about your painting?

Yes. For instance, I drew a picture of a girl who has very pretty, long legs and long red hair, pretty face, beautiful body, and she is in a very short dress. She's winding up to throw a baseball, standing up like this and there's drool coming out of the side of her mouth and it's called *Spitball*. I just wanted to juxtapose her beauty with that kind of boy stuff. I figure if it amuses me maybe it will amuse somebody else.

Do you go through the same process with painting as you do writing a lyric?

It's very similar. It's a different form of communication, but whoever Grace is comes out in my paintings. This gallery was showing a grouping of maybe thirty of my pictures, so I went around and looked at them and thought, "Boy, not very subtle." I'm just not very subtle. But you can't help being yourself, you know, it's just "there I am."

Was that your attitude toward your music as well?

I always like to watch it happen. Usually I'd come in and play the band a song I'd written on the guitar or piano. I wouldn't tell them what to do—just here's the song. Then Jack would decide to do whatever and Jorma would do what he did. Marty would say, "I want to put this in here," okay, fine. And then you'd watch that song, that piece of communication being built into something big, kind of the same way gossip is built in pieces, only it's not behind your back.

Do you like the idea that painting is something you just do by yourself?

I'm not a really good enough musician so I can't put in a "background" like I can in painting. You see, my songs are more like sketches. In a sense, I'm just putting down a few colors and lines that need to be completed. My agent might say, "See this picture of Jerry Garcia you painted? I want you to do four of them right next to each other like a Warhol thing, and I want one in soft green, one in red, and blah-blah-blah." Well, fine, I don't care because the original picture to me is done. With writing, the song is done, but then it still becomes this other thing, which is so much fun to watch happen. And I don't mind at all because we're all in the business together and we have the same intent, which is to make this piece of work as acceptable as possible to the public. If someone comes up with a better way for the subject matter to pop out, it doesn't matter to me. Once I draw or paint that initial image, once I've written a song lyric, a melody, or chords, then you can do whatever you want and it's fine by me, because for me, it's already done. I just like hearing other people add to and interpret what I put out there.

Were there any people who influenced your life that you never got a chance to talk to?

Miles Davis. I once took acid and listened to the *Sketches of Spain* album by Miles Davis and Gil Evans. I listened to it for twenty-four hours, over and over and over again. After that, whenever I sat down with a guitar or piano I'd have to literally tell myself, "Okay, just don't make it feel 'Spanish.'" But sometimes those brain chemicals get together and it just happens. See, "White Rabbit" is a Spanish march. It's partly from Miles Davis's *Sketches of Spain* and partly other stuff, too, but the beauty in that recording was the way Miles and Gil Evans intertwined American jazz and a Spanish feel, however you want to describe it. I had never heard anything like it before or since.

Do you think celebrity brings a lot of baggage with it that people aren't aware of?

Sure, but that's what the deal is this time around. You know, you can't get too pushed out of shape about the baggage that comes with any job. Like getting really famous and complaining about people following you around, taking your picture, like it isn't in the job description. You didn't know that? Some people seem so surprised by the downside of celebrity. And I say, "Well, what did you think was going to happen?" It's just life. I don't like brushing my teeth either but I do it because I don't want them to fall out.

Grace Slick performinmg with Starship, 1985

Do you think people have a hard time separating you from their memory of Jefferson Airplane?

Oh, sure. The Airplane is still everyone's first impression of me and that was a couple of decades ago. The Airplane came from a time when the kids, everybody, knew all the bands that were out there at the time. Now there are thousands of them. It's a different era and you really have to stand out now. You've got to do the Madonna thing and change your clothes every five minutes and have weird hair color and dancers and exploding chickens and everything else just to get noticed. Except for Dave Matthews. He's just a regular guy, it's a regular band, and they just blew me away. I went to see him and just stood up for two and a half hours. There was nothing really going on but good old rock and roll and that was so nice for a change.

So do you think the world has any misconceptions about Grace Slick?

I don't think there are any misconceptions because every perception is correct. Who am I to say your perception is wrong? And who are you to say mine is? We're all just doing this dance and it's all just fine.

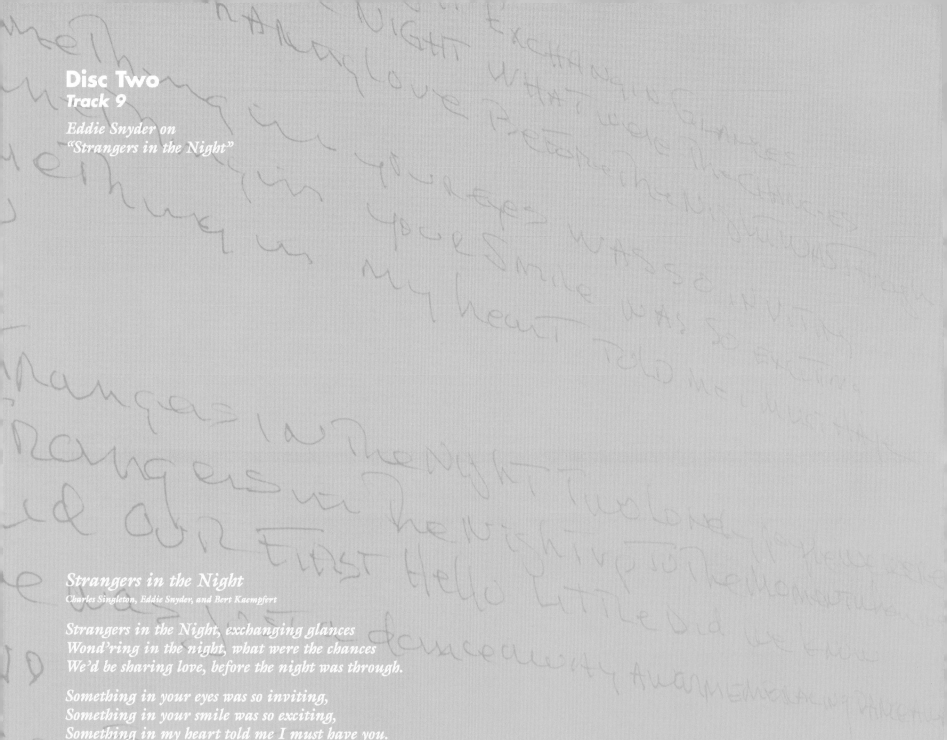

Eddie Snyder on
"Strangers in the Night"

Strangers in the Night

Charles Singleton, Eddie Snyder, and Bert Kaempfert

Strangers in the Night, exchanging glances
Wond'ring in the night, what were the chances
We'd be sharing love, before the night was through.

Something in your eyes was so inviting,
Something in your smile was so exciting,
Something in my heart told me I must have you.

Strangers in the Night, two lonely people
We were Strangers in the Night
Up to the moment when we said our first hello, little did we know
Love was just a glance away, a warm embracing dance away.

Ever since that night, we've been together.
Lovers at first sight, in love forever.
It turned out so right, for Strangers in the Night.

Chapter 21

Eddie Snyder

"STRANGERS IN THE NIGHT"

STRANGERS IN THE NIGHT EXCHANGIN GLANCES
WONDERING IN THE NIGHT WHAT WERE THE CHANCES
WE'D BE SHARING LOVE BEFORE THE NIGHT WAS THROUGH

SOMETHING IN YOUR EYES WAS SO INVITING
SOMETHING IN YOUR SMILE WAS SO EXCITING
SOMETHING IN MY HEART TOLD ME I MUST HAVE
YOU

STRANGERS IN THE NIGHT TWO LONELY PEOPLE WE WERE
STRANGERS IN THE NIGHT UP TO THE MOMENT WHEN WE
SAID OUR FIRST HELLO LITTLE DID WE KNOW
LOVE WAS JUST A DANCE AWAY A WARM EMBRACING DANCE AWAY
AND

EVER SINCE THAT NIGHT WE'VE BEEN TOGETHER
LOVERS AT FIRST SIGHT IN LOVE FOREVER
IT TURNED OUT SO RIGHT FOR
FOR STRANGERS IN THE NIGHT
DOOBY DOOBY DO

Eddie Snyder

164

"In the sixties, I was a 'writing factory,' and practically turning out a song a day. . . . You'd write all day and then play it for somebody, and if they decided to take the song, then fine. If not, then you'd take it across the street and play it there."

"We looked at songwriting as a nine-to-five, seven-days-a-week business and the publishers were the clients. If he wanted it blue, then we said, 'Blue it is.'"

Frank Sinatra

"Strangers in the Night," written by Charles Singleton, Eddie Snyder, and Bert Kaempfert, was recorded by Frank Sinatra for Reprise Records in 1966. It was on Billboard's Hot 100 *for eleven weeks and reached #1. Receiving five Grammy nominations that year, it won four, including Record of the Year and Best Vocal Performance, Male. BMI awarded "Strangers in the Night" a Citation of Achievement for reaching more than five million broadcast performances. Eddie Snyder now makes his home in central Florida.*

I was born in 1919 on the East Side of New York City, along with many other famous people like George and Ira Gershwin. But when I was quite young, my folks moved up to Harlem, which of course is now all black but at that time was a Jewish neighborhood as well.

Do you feel the time and place that you were born had much influence on your musical outlook?

My father had a good singing voice and one of my grandparents, whom I never met, wrote songs. We never met because he didn't survive the Holocaust. I believe that in some way, all of these things have their own effect, so perhaps rather than being influenced by the time and place that I was born, maybe whatever talent I possess was somehow transmitted through the genes.

Do you think that songwriting is mainly a product of inspiration?

In the sixties, I was a "writing factory" and practically turning out a song a day. That's simply how I was making a living. You'd write all day and then play it for somebody, and if they decided to take the song, then fine. If not, then you'd take it across the street and play it there. And if they took the song, then my partner and I, Charlie Singleton, would wind up getting roughly a hundred dollars, which wasn't bad for a day's work.

Was it hard to make a living in those days as a songwriter?

I remember one Friday came along and I said to Charlie, who was a very talented writer and with whom I cowrote "Spanish Eyes" and "Strangers in the Night," "If we don't pick up any money we're going to be in trouble over the weekend." And that's how we came to write "Trouble Over the Weekend." We probably got one hundred dollars for that song. Another time, we had a hard time finding anyone who wanted what we had written so we went across the street to the Goodman brothers, as in Benny Goodman, and they took all four of our songs. It was always a gamble.

Can you remember the first time you heard something you had written on the radio?

It was "A Hundred Pounds of Clay." Do you remember that? I don't know how many times I've heard one of my songs being performed, but it's a thrill every time.

Do you have any kind of set routine which helps you with your writing?

Eddie Snyder met his wife, Jessie, in 1947 at the McFadden Deauville Hotel in Miami, Florida, where she sang with the society band and he played piano in another room. They were married five weeks later and have been together for sixty-five years.

I do a lot of walking. I'm not doing as much as I did a few years ago, but if I'm working, then I'm walking. But I don't think there's a formula at all. There was one time when I had started a song with a partner of mine who then went down to Miami. He liked the melody and had left me to work out the lyrics. So I walked and walked and walked. By the time he got back, I had the song finished and it was a beautiful song called "Save a Place for Me." In my case, if I charged by the mile, and not by the song, I'd probably be a wealthy man today.

Is getting your songs placed with the right artist a difficult process?

I was playing piano once at a bar where a lot of important music people came when they were in town from New York. You know, publishers and that kind of thing. One of these guys heard "The Girl with the Golden Braids" and asked for a copy of it. Well, he got it to Perry Como, who recorded it and did a wonderful job on it. It's not that easy today. A couple of years later, I was singing a song that had become very popular with the people who came into the Lorraine Room at the Fontainebleau Hotel. This one day, I had just finished playing it and Andy Williams came over to the piano and said, "What's that?" I said, "It's an original song called 'Talk to Me.'" Out of the blue, he asked me to send it to him, which I did. The long and the short of it is that Sinatra ended up recording it.

Are some songs easier to write than others?

When I came up to New York in 1961, I had this one particular title in mind for a song that I had been carrying around for a while. There are some days I'll write down as many as a hundred titles and file them away, sometimes for years. Then you come across that title again and you go, "Oh yeah, that would be perfect for this or that." And this time it was kind of like that. The title was "A Hundred Pounds of Clay." My partner and I came across this title and sat down in the basement at the piano with no melody and no lyrics and within twenty minutes we had a song that became a top ten hit. All of it came from the title. The process is always different. Sometimes it just happens that way.

Is it more difficult to write on demand?

You never know. As I said, Charlie and I were like factory workers—we just kept churning them out. We worked in this little airless, windowless room every day, nine to five. Hal Fine, the music publisher, was right across the hall from us and through our closed door, every day for two years, we had been hearing this melody coming from across the hall. It was like torture, because we couldn't stand what we were hearing. It was just the same three chords over and over, and since I had gone to Juilliard, I knew at least five chords [laughs]. It was particularly hard for me. So one day Hal Fine called me and Charlie into his office and told us for that for two years he had tried to get some of the best writers in the country to

Jessie and Eddie Snyder in 1972 at their "retirement" home in Avon Park, Florida, with some of Eddie's awards

come up with lyrics for this Bert Kaempfert melody, and so far, nothing made him happy. So he had called us in. He started to play the instrumental version of the song and Charlie and I asked, "Do you have a title for this?" He told us it was "Spanish Arms." We thought about it and then all of a sudden, Charlie says, "Spanish Eyes." And that immediately sparked the idea for the lyrics. So in about an hour we came back with the lyrics to "Spanish Eyes." I get a kick out of telling that story because it's just amazing how the good Lord or God or whatever you want to call him arranges for things to happen the way they do. As it turned out, we got Al Martino and both he and Hal Fine were very happy with the way "Spanish Eyes" turned out. "Strangers in the Night" was another Bert Kaempfert melody that was used in a bomb of a movie with James Garner and Melina Mercouri called *A Man Could Get Killed*. They played the song throughout the picture and Frank Sinatra sang the song over the credits at the end. I thought we might have qualified for an Academy Award for Best Song that year, but nobody bothered to enter it. That's the way it goes sometimes, but we were just happy to have a hit. So those were the two biggest hits we had, "Spanish Eyes" and "Strangers in the Night." I've been a bum ever since those two songs.

You've written under several different names. What was the reason for that?

There was a time when I was an ASCAP writer, and I still am. The rules are that you can't write with someone who's a member of BMI. George Pincus, the publisher, asked me if I would go as a BMI writer, so I wrote under a bunch of different names, Kaye Rogers, Edward A. Snyder, and Eddie Snyder; all of those are me. I wrote "A Hundred Pounds of Clay," as Kaye Rogers. That was the name my wife, Jesse, was singing under when I first met her, so we used it to get around the ASCAP-BMI thing.

At the time I was working with Stanley Kahn. Stanley was connected with the Shirelles and Florence Greenberg, the woman who managed them. Florence had a very disreputable character as a partner named Luther Dixon. When he first heard "A Hundred Pounds of Clay" he thought it needed something else and asked, "Can't you write another little thing here?" You remember the part "Can't you just see him walking 'round and 'round / picking the clay up off the ground." Well, we didn't have that at first. That was for Luther, and what the hell, it took all of five minutes. Stanley was brilliant that way. I sat down at the piano and played the chords and Stanley came up with the words. I had given him the title maybe two years before in Miami and he said, "Eddie, don't you forget that title." So here we were two years later banging out an extra lyric for Luther Dixon. Some writers might mind but you have to understand, we looked at songwriting as a nine-to-five, seven-days-a-week business and the publisher was the client. If he wanted it blue, then we said, "Blue it is." If he wanted it red, well, you get the picture. At the time I thought it would be a good song for Pat Boone. He was committed to record it, which we were pretty happy about because he was a big star and we were sure it would be a huge hit for him. I never found out why he didn't record it. Anyway, Snuffy Garrett, who produced the song, got it to Gene McDaniels, who did record it and it went to #3 in the charts. Not bad, huh? When it got to #3 I said, "Who's Pat Boone, anyway?" On principle, because I wrote it, I never went out and bought a copy so I only ever heard it a couple of times on the radio. They still play it now and then. Just last week, I got a $563 royalty check for it. That's a quarterly check, so it still makes a couple of thousand a year.

Do you have any thoughts on the current state of songwriting today?

These days, I try and write country songs. In my opinion, that's where the very finest writers are creating the best songs. I'd like to try to have another couple hits and as far as I can tell, Nashville is the only place left for true American music. I've been immersing myself in country music these days, especially on the weekends when they play the top forty. But in general terms, I'll write to whatever my partner comes up with melodically. One thing I do feel is that I'm writing as well as I did in the 1960s, maybe even better.

How has the business changed over the years?

More competitive. I talked with the guy who manages EMI in Nashville and he has forty staff writers, forty! Sony Music Publishing, and some of the others I would have to guess, would have ten or fifteen writers each on staff. One would have to write another "Star Spangled Banner" to compete with that.

Do you have any advice for up-and-coming songwriters?

I would say, screw around with it. Ask yourself, is songwriting something you like, or is it something you love? Is it something you want to do all your life? Do you feel compelled to do it or is it just a hobby? I'd tell them "If you love it, good, then write." If you want to get involved seriously in the craft, then you have to be prepared to pick up your roots and go to where the business is, places like New York, Nashville, L.A., wherever. And bring money and luck and a sense of humor, because you'll need them.

Eddie and his wife Jessie, Christmas, 1995

Disc Two
Track 10

Billy Steinberg on
"True Colors"

True Colors
Billy Steinberg and Tom Kelly

You with the sad eyes
Don't be discouraged
Oh I realize
It's hard to take courage
In a world full of people
You can lose sight of it all
And the darkness inside you
Can make you feel so small

But I see your true colors
Shining through
I see your true colors
And that's why I love you
So don't be afraid to let them show
Your true colors
True colors are beautiful
Like a rainbow

Show me a smile then,
Don't be unhappy, can't remember
When I last saw you laughing
If this world makes you crazy
And you've taken all you can bear
You call me up
Because you know I'll be there

And I'll see your true colors
Shining through
I see your true colors
And that's why I love you.
So don't be afraid to let them show
Your true colors

True colors are beautiful
Like a rainbow.

Chapter 22

Billy Steinberg / Tom Kelly

PHOTO: MELANIE NISSEN/MONTAGE

true colors

you with the sad eyes
   don't be discouraged
      oh, i realize it's hard to find courage
      in a world full of people
         you can lose sight of it all
            and the darkness inside you
               makes you feel so small

but i see your true colors shining through
   i see your true colors
      that's why i love you
         don't be afraid to let them show
            your true colors ... your true colors
               are as beautiful as a rainbow

show me a smile then
   don't be unhappy
      can't remember when i last saw you laughing
      if this world makes you crazy
         and you're taken all you can bear
            call for me, baby
               and you know i'll be there

Billy Steinberg   *Tom Kelly*

"Before I met Tom Kelly, I wrote my own songs, both words and music, and I thought I was pretty good at both. But when I began to work with Tom, it was instantly obvious that here was a guy with a true gift for melody which made my own abilities in that area pale."

"There weren't many girls you could sit down and read poetry to, but if you said, 'I just wrote this song, you wanna hear it?,' you were in."

Cyndi Lauper

PHOTO: ROBERT CORWIN

"True Colors," written by Billy Steinberg and Tom Kelly, was recorded by Cyndi Lauper for Portrait Records in 1986. It stayed on Billboard's Hot 100 *for twelve weeks and held the #1 spot for two weeks. It has been recorded by Phil Collins, appeared in the feature film* Save the Last Dance, *and used by Kodak in a series of commercials. This song was on the* True Colors *album, which has since gone multi-platinum. Billy Steinberg and Tom Kelly live in Los Angeles, California.*

The following is an interview with Billy Steinberg.

I was born in Fresno, California, on February 26, 1950. Fresno is in the heart of the San Joaquin Valley, where my dad was a farmer. In 1958, he moved our family to the Coachella Valley and I grew up in Palm Springs.

Do you think where you were born and raised had an influence on your music?

Absolutely. Just lately, I've realized that when you listen to the great songs of the sixties and seventies, you can tell which of those writers were influenced by the music of the fifties. Even though they're one or two decades removed, you can hear little "tips of the hat" to that music. Now it's 2002 and there are a lot of songs on the radio written by people who didn't grow up with the songs of the fifties at all and their songs don't show a trace of the fifties melodic or lyrical sensibilities. The very first songs that had a real impact on me were part of an older friend's record collection. My first record player was primarily made for playing forty-fives. If you put an album on the turntable, it hung out over the sides like pancakes that were too big for the plate. I'd listen to my small but growing collection of forty-fives over and over and over and I know my father thought there was something wrong with me. The very first songs that I remember I had were "Poor Little Fool" by Ricky Nelson, "Little Star" by the Elegants, "All I Have to Do Is Dream" by the Everly Brothers, and "Young Love" by Sonny James. Actually I lied, the cool version was by Sonny James; I had the Tab Hunter version. Those were some of the early songs I loved, and when I started writing, those songs were right there in my mind.

Are you more motivated to write because of inspiration or dedication?

A different proportion thereof. You see, it's not that difficult to write a good song; what's difficult is to write a great song. I've probably written close to a thousand songs but there are just a handful of them that I'm proud of, that measure up to my favorite songs. If you look back on the songs of the fifties and sixties, you'll see the same names over and over: Burt Bacharach and Hal David, Gerry Goffin and Carole King, Smokey Robinson or Holland-Dozier-Holland. You see those names on a lot of the songs that have endured. That's why my answer is, it isn't 99 percent perspiration, because a lot of people are willing to perspire. Sure, you have to work hard to be good at it, but you also have to have the gift and one of those gifts also has to be the ability to accept rejection. There basically are two types of people: those who are devastated by rejection and those who are fueled by it. I'm definitely the latter.

Do you have a special routine which helps you write?

Billy Steinberg and Tom Kelly in Tom's home studio in Woodland Hills, California, 1989

PHOTO: RITA MAGIDSON

Maybe this will answer the question. I started out loving records as we discussed. I remember as a kid being utterly mystified by the fact that my friends didn't love records as much as I did. When I tried to sit them down to listen to a record, they just didn't have that passion in their eyes and it disappointed me. I couldn't ever find anyone, as a child, to share that with. So it became my secret world of songs. By the time I got to junior high the Beatles, the Rolling Stones, the Kinks, and the Animals were happening, so I got in a band. We were called the Fables and we had little business cards that read THE FABULOUS FABLES. We used to cover all the great songs of the time. It never occurred to me when I was in the Fables that we could write our own songs. There was a kid named Danny I knew at Palm Springs High School who had made a record. It wasn't bad either but, of course, it went nowhere. But it implanted the idea in my brain, "Oh, you could write a song and make a record." I never did write a song for the Fabulous Fables or my next band, Dirt, either. In my later years of high school, I had my poems printed in a little student writers' booklet. All the students and parents got a copy and that was exciting to me. But it never occurred to me to combine the music I was playing in the bands with the poetry I was writing. When I got to Bard College in 1968, I started to write "folky" type songs to the poetry I was writing. Once I started to do that, I got totally hooked on songwriting. A lot of it was, of course, ego driven. There weren't many girls you could sit down and read poetry to, but if you said, "I just wrote this song, you wanna hear it?," you were in. I was sort of a flower child in the late sixties, so I would say my very first songs were influenced by Donovan and Tim Buckley, and some of the gentler writers.

Do the words or music come to you first?

Ninety-nine percent of the songs I've written have been written with the lyrics first. For me, the lyric informs the music and even when I met Tom Kelly in 1981, I kind of converted him to that method. I was very fortunate that he liked my arriving with lyrics already done, so it's always been the lyrics first.

Has any one song been tougher to write than any of the others?

You mean the hardest to write? "True Colors" was the hardest song I ever wrote. I wrote a verse and a chorus lyric and then I got together with Tom [Kelly] and we put it to music. Tom played the music and wrote most of the melody on the spot, and it flowed out easy. But then, lo and behold, Tom and I agreed that my original verse lyric was too specific, while the chorus was universal. So I had to rewrite the lyrics to the first and second verses. It took forever to rewrite that song. Frankly, at that point in my career, I didn't know how to rewrite a song. Early on, I had a band called Billy Thermal and we were signed to Richard Perry's label, Planet Records. I remember one time after playing a demo for Perry he said to me, "Do you always just put down the first thing that comes into your mind, or do you rewrite?" I could feel my blood begin to boil, and I guess I felt threatened, because, of course, I never rewrote anything; I didn't know how. He told me that Carly Simon had written verse upon verse of "You're So Vain" and sorted through what she had written and picked the best ones. I thought to myself, "Who cares what Carly Simon did!" I was so mad. Even though I liked the song, I just didn't like being told that. At the time, I just felt threatened because I didn't know how to do what he was asking, but now I do.

Billy Steinberg and Cyndi Lauper traveling with a special group of American songwriters in the Soviet Union, November 1988

Was there anyone in your life whom you felt driven to succeed for?

I had a burning desire to prove something to myself and so I was very self-motivated. I'd say if there was anyone who I wanted to succeed for it would have been my father. My dad made his living as a farmer and that was his career. It was a passion of his and his hobby was politics. He had it all planned out in his mind that farming would be my career and that songwriting would be to me the same as politics was to him—a hobby. He definitely encouraged my songwriting, but I wanted to prove to him that songwriting wasn't just going to be a hobby. My dad's second wife knew Jann Wenner at *Rolling Stone* magazine and unbeknownst to me, had sent him some of my early demo tapes. I never heard his comments directly, but she told me he said my songs were "okay." "Okay"? What could be more devastating? There wasn't even a flicker of hope there. But all those little disappointments would fuel me, and so I thought, "I'm going to show those bastards."

When was the first time you felt you were starting to have some success?

For me it was a big leap. I had a band called Billy Thermal and the guitar player knew Linda Ronstadt. He didn't ask or tell me, but he played her a tape of our early demos. I was told she loved a song called "How Do I Make You?" and apparently wanted to record it. I had already dealt with so much rejection in my life that I said, "Yeah, sure she does." I wasn't being a pessimist; I just didn't want to be devastated by yet another disappointment. Shortly thereafter, there was an article in the *L.A. Times* reviewing a fund-raising concert Linda [Ronstadt] had done for Jerry Brown. It read, as I remember it, "Linda Ronstadt performs some of her new material, the strongest of which was the song 'How Do I Make You?'" Sure enough, when her album *Mad Love* came out, the single was "How Do I Make You?" and it became a top ten hit. That was my first cover and it wedged my foot firmly in the door.

Where were you when you first heard one of your songs on the radio?

I was working in my dad's vineyards where we employed crews of day laborers who used to play transistor radios as they worked. The first time I ever heard "How Do I Make You?" it started playing on one of the worker's radios and I just wanted to scream, "I wrote that song!" But there was no one to scream it to, so I just sort of grinned like a Cheshire cat for the rest of the day.

Was there anyone who influenced your music whom you wish you had met?

I guess I would have to say Bob Dylan and John Lennon are my two biggest heroes. I never met John Lennon. I met Bob Dylan briefly and I tried to have a conversation; I tried. You know, when you worship someone as much as I do these two immense talents, it would be hard to have a satisfying conversation. Like a lot of other people, I'm fascinated by the mystery of Robert Johnson. I've read about Johnson, Charlie Patton, and some of the great pre-war blues singers and I often wonder what the 1930s rural Mississippi world that they inhabited must have been like and that fascinates me. Chuck Berry is another guy who's one of my great heroes.

Was there someone along the way who tried to trample on your dreams?

No, one person doesn't come to mind, but in the late seventies, when I was working out in the vineyards, which is a good two-hour drive from Los Angeles, I used to try my hardest to make connections in the business here in L.A. Whether it was a record company executive or a publishing company guy, I used to somehow get appointments. So I'd get in my pickup truck and drive the couple of hours it took to get to L.A. Foolishly, I would look forward to those meetings weeks in advance. I'd get there right on time and be sitting in the waiting room and let's say, maybe my appointment was at one o'clock. Then two o'clock would roll by, then two-thirty, and finally the guy would walk in the door. The secretary would say, "Here's your phone messages," and invariably hand him a satchel full of messages. Then he would shuffle through them and say to me, "I'll just be another minute, I have to return this call." Or even worse, I'd go into his office and he would throw on my little demo tape and then make his phone calls while my tape was playing. I could see the guy's not listening to my tape; either that or he's got the volume dialed down. The phone call ends, he says he's sorry, and maybe he rewinds the tape, maybe not. And within a few minutes I'm standing on the street corner thinking, "What the hell am I doing this for?" Over the years, there've been a lot of those guys. But as much as I remember people like that, I also remember all the people who liked what I was trying to do and helped me.

Any advice in particular you might give to an aspiring songwriter?

First I would say it's quality not quantity. If I were to chart the income of all the songs I've written, I'd say, and I'm just throwing a number out here, that ninety percent of the money I've made has been off of five percent of the songs. Take "True Colors" for instance. There was the hit with Cyndi Lauper and then Phil Collins covered it. It was used in the movie *Save the Last Dance* and then Kodak used it for a series of TV commercials; it just doesn't stop. My advice would be to focus on what you're doing because nobody's going to reward you for how many songs you write. That's one bit of advice. Another piece of advice would be to stay open to the self-knowledge of both what you have to offer and what you're lacking. For instance, before I met Tom Kelly, I wrote my own songs, both words and music, and I thought I was pretty good at both. But when I began to work with Tom, it was instantly obvious that here was a guy with a true gift for melody which made my own abilities in that area pale. So, my advice to an aspiring songwriter would be: Be proud of what you do well, but don't be too proud to not know what you don't.

George David Weiss on
"What a Wonderful World"

What a Wonderful World

George David Weiss and Bob Thiele

I see trees of green, red roses too,
I see them bloom, for me and you,
And I think to myself, WHAT A WONDERFUL WORLD.

I see skies of blue, and clouds of white,
The bright blessed day, the dark sacred night,
And I think to myself, WHAT A WONDERFUL WORLD.

The colors of the rainbow so pretty in the sky,
Are also on the faces of people goin' by;
I see friends shakin' hands, sayin', "How do you do!"
They're really sayin', "I love you."

I hear babies cry, I watch them grow;
They'll learn much more than I'll ever know,
And I think to myself, WHAT A WONDERFUL WORLD.
Yes, I think to myself, WHAT A WONDERFUL WORLD.

Chapter 23

George David Weiss

"WHAT A WONDERFUL WORLD"

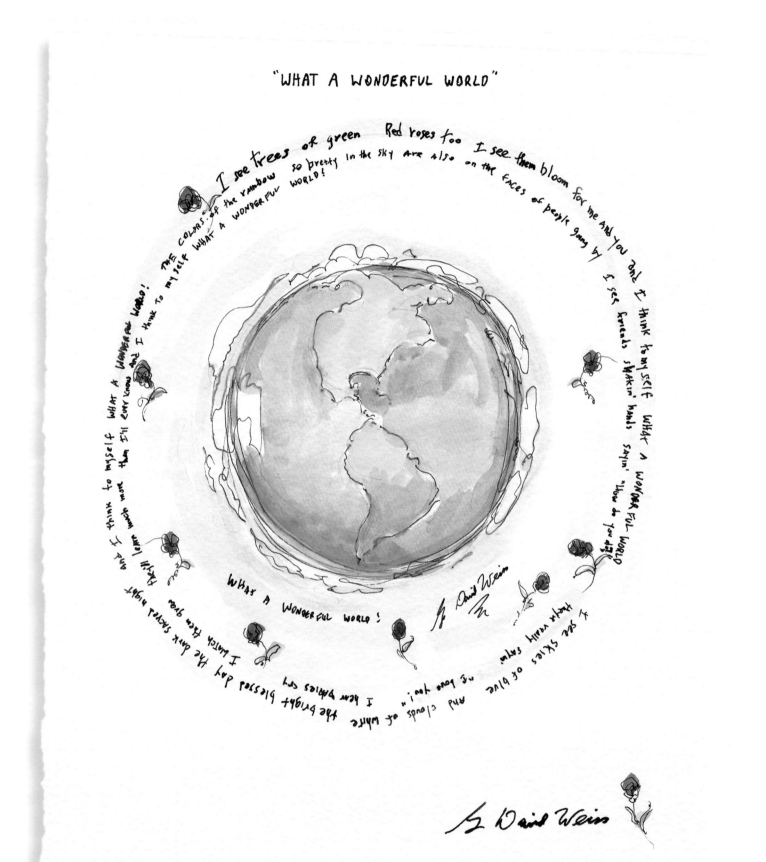

I see trees of green   Red roses too   I see them bloom for me and you and I think to myself   WHAT A WONDERFUL WORLD   I see skies of blue   And clouds of white   the bright blessed day   the dark sacred night   And I think to myself   WHAT A WONDERFUL WORLD!   THE COLORS of the rainbow   so pretty in the sky   Are also   on the faces of people going by   I see friends shakin' hands sayin' "How do you do"   They're really sayin' "I love you"   I hear babies cry   I watch them grow   They'll learn much more   than I'll ever know   and I think to myself   WHAT A WONDERFUL WORLD!

180

"I always wait for the inspiration, for an idea to come and slam me down into the street. You know, just absolutely slam me down and knock me out."

"We presented it to the head of the publishing company and he said, 'Oh, it's very nice, but we want another 'Hound Dog.'"

Louis Armstrong

"What a Wonderful World," written by George David Weiss and Bob Thiele, was recorded by Louis Armstrong for Decca Records in 1967. Not until its appearance in the feature film Good Morning, Vietnam *and its subsequent rerelease on the film's A&M Records soundtrack in 1988, did it become a* Billboard *Top 40 hit. Louis Armstrong received a Grammy Hall of Fame Award for his recording of the song in 1999. A past-president of the Songwriters Guild of America, George David Weiss was inducted into the Songwriters Hall of Fame in 1984. He divides his time between his homes in Oldwick, New Jersey, and Cabo San Lucas, Mexico.*

I grew up in New York City when pop music was virtually in its ascendancy, and when I say "pop music," I'm really referring to the music that was coming out of movies and the great songs that were coming out of Broadway.

Were there specific songs or movies that struck you as being inspirational at the time?

I don't know. I'd hesitate to try to pick out one specific song or show. It was simply an experience of being deeply immersed in that world of music; all of those songs and great songwriters really had an effect on me.

When you were just starting out in this profession, was there anyone in particular you wanted to succeed for besides yourself?

Actually, I had a lot of trouble with my mother, who was very concerned and didn't want me to go into such an unpredictable, unforgiving business. But I didn't have any problems at all with my dad. He was always on my side. He was always saying to my mother, "Rae, why don't you leave the kid alone? Let him do what he wants. Leave him alone."

Was your father a music fan?

Actually, he wasn't. He wasn't a musician, but what did motivate him to encourage me was his deep sense of "human beingness," as it were.

What was his profession?

He was a milkman and worked for Sheffield Farms for all those years. Eventually, I think because of me, he opened a little sheet music and secondhand record shop on Broadway and Forty-ninth Street. At first, he just sold secondhand records, and then later, new releases. It all happened because, believe it or not, I had inspired him.

When was the first time you felt you had reached some degree of success? Was it hearing something of yours on the radio?

The first time I actually heard something I had written on the radio, it was Frank Sinatra singing a sensational rendition of "Oh! What It Seemed to Be." That was the very first time, and unbelievably, it was also the number one record on the charts.

Had you been writing songs prior to that?

Oh yes, I had started writing when I was a child. I just loved writing so much I could hardly stand it when I had to stop and go to school or even eat, for that matter.

When you're writing, do you think first in words or in music?

Well, most of the time I compose either in my head or at the piano. I guess it's fair to say I think both in words and music almost simultaneously but perhaps a little bit faster on the lyric end.

Can you explain how inspiration comes to you? Does it come in the form of a melody or fragment of a lyric?

Generally, I just start with a simple thought. In the case of "Oh! What It Seemed to Be" for instance, that song started with my having the thought, "What does one do when one meets somebody? How does a romance begin, how does it go forward?" That thought then became the beginning of a story in the form of a lyric. "It was just a neighborhood dance, that's all that it was / But oh! What it seemed to be!" That was how that song started.

So when you have a lyric roughed out, do you then sit down at the piano and fashion a melody?

No, in this case I was working with Bennie Benjamin, who had already had two or three prior hits. We had met in my father's music shop where he had heard a few of my early attempts at writing. To this day, and I still don't really know why, he decided to ask me if I would team up with him. I laughed my head off and said, "Bennie, what's the matter with you, are you crazy? You've had hit songs already and I'm nobody. What do you mean you want to write with me?" And he said, "Well, I've seen your early efforts and I know talent when I see it. You have talent and I think we could both do great." I thought he was nuts, I really did, but he kept insisting that I at least try to work with him. He even went to my parents and asked, "What's wrong with your son? I want to work with him and he keeps telling me 'no.'" After that, my dad got a hold of me and said in his usual warm and loving way, "George, what's wrong? What's the matter with you?" I told him, "How could I take advantage of this man? I'm just a rank amateur." He looked at me and said firmly, "Oh, no, you're not. You're a professional." My father, of course, was right. He was so sweet, so good, and he did everything he could to make me see that if I wanted to, I possibly could have a shot at this writing thing. So I finally said I would give it a try. The next day I came up with the lyric "It was just a neighborhood dance, that's all that it was / But oh! What it seemed to be!" I called Bennie up and asked him what he thought and he just went crazy over it and said "Oh, my God, George, that's so original." Then I knew I had a shot at this. The next day, I found myself walking up and down the street with Bennie outside of the Brill Building in Manhattan polishing the lyric. We sang each other silly, just trying to sort out the melody. People were looking at us like we were crazy.

Would you say this would be an example of a song being 1 percent inspiration and 99 percent perspiration?

I find that the perspiration comes after the inspiration. I always wait for the inspiration, for an idea to come and slam me down into the street. You know, just absolutely slam me down and knock me out. That's when the perspiration begins, because it's at that point I really start working and hopefully something will come out of it.

Is there anything you do to put yourself in a creative mood?

No, never. I just wait for it. When I have an idea, I'll write from nine to five or however long it takes. But in terms of waiting for that idea or for inspiration, I just go out and live my life and hope that something occurs.

What would you say are your strengths and weaknesses as a songwriter?

Let me put it this way: If there are any real weak points I have, it would have to be that I'm too impatient with myself. Once I get the idea and it's starting to flow, it's like, "Come on, let's go, let's hear it already." I'd say that's a weak point. If I could say I have a strong point, it would be that I eventually overcome that impatient urge, get down to it, and work and work until I'm actually satisfied. In the background, I'll always hear my dad telling me, "George, have confidence and keep going. You'll get it, you'll see." I've never not "heard" or "seen" my dad, and to this day, I still see him and hear his words all the time. I've always said this and I think it is always true: "If you still have a relationship with that person, then how can they ever actually be gone?"

Have you ever written a song for your dad?

It's been almost as if everything I have done has really been because of him, and in a way, was for him as well. Was there anything specific? Not yet, but who knows.

What was his proudest moment that he enjoyed with you?

Actually, it was when I got that first song of mine recorded and saw it become the #1 song on the *Hit Parade*. You should have seen how he decorated the window of the shop. What a man he was! What a lovely and kind man.

Do you think the public is aware of the writers that produce classic songs such as yours?

There are certainly plenty of people who don't know me and like many writers, have not heard of me. Perhaps that's my own fault, because I never was interested in public relations, as it were. So when I started to "make it," so to speak, I didn't go around crowing, "Look, look at me. Look what I just wrote." It never would have occurred to me. It was never what this has been about for me.

"Can't Help Falling in Love with You" was a huge hit for Elvis. Is there a story behind that song?

I recall very clearly how it came about. It was a song that Hugo [Peretti], Luigi [Creatore], and I wrote together, and not for any particular project. It was just a song we thought would be well suited for Elvis in general. We presented it to the head of the publishing company and he said, "Oh, it's very nice, but we want another 'Hound Dog.' And he meant it, boy, he was banging his fist on the table and ranting, "Give me another 'Hound Dog!' I said, "Look, this is what we wrote because we believe in him, we believe in his voice, and we believe he can make this ballad his own. Why don't you just play the tape for him and see what he thinks. Send it to him and let him decide." He begrudgingly said, "Well, all right," and he did, but he was very unconvinced. Well, weeks went by, and frankly, I forgot all about it. Then out of the blue, I heard back from the company that Elvis had quite accidentally heard the song. Apparently, Elvis was walking down a hallway and he went past this room where his sycophants were listening to songs that might be used in an upcoming picture he was scheduled to do called *Blue Hawaii*. I'm told he stood at the doorway and asked "What was that y'all are playing?" They told him, "It's nothing to get excited about. It's just a lousy little ballad." He said he wanted to hear it again and stood by that door while they played it over and over and over. He kept repeating, "I love that song. I want to do it in my movie." So they said, "Well, okay, if you really think so." He said, "Yes, I think so!" So they put it aside but in no way wanted it included in the picture. At Elvis's insistence they tested the movie including the song. Apparently it worked very well, but it was completely unexpected. The long and short of it is, the sales of the single topped a million just because of the song, wow! And the punch line is, "Can't Help Falling in Love with You" was only the "B" side of the single, because they never put a ballad on the "A" side of any of Elvis's records. It just goes to show, you can't say no to the public.

Would you have any words of wisdom or advice for an aspiring songwriter?

Patience, patience, patience. Think about it and wait for the answers to come.

Disc Two
Track 12

Paul Williams on
"We've Only Just Begun"

We've Only Just Begun
Roger Nichols and Paul Williams

We've only just begun to live
White lace and promises
A kiss for luck and we're on our way

Before the rising sun we fly
So many roads to choose
We start out walking and learn to run
And yes, we've just begun

Sharing horizons that are new to us
Watching the signs along the way
Talking it over just the two of us
Working together day to day
Together.

And when the evening comes we smile
So much of life ahead
We'll find a place where there's room to grow
And yes, we've just begun
We've only just begun

Chapter 24

Paul Williams

PHOTO: JIM McCRARY

'WE'VE ONLY JUST BEGUN'

We've only just begun to live
White lace & promises
a kiss for luck
And we're on our way

Before the rising sun
We fly

So many roads to choose
We start out walking
And learn to run
And 'yes' we've just begun

Sharing horizons that are
new to us
Watching the signs along the way —
Talking it over just the two of us
Working together Day by day — & Together

And when the evening comes we smile
So much of life ahead —
We'll find a place where there's room to grow
And yes we've just begun
We've only just begun

Paul Williams

"'We've Only Just Begun' had all the romantic beginnings of a bank commercial. Really, Roger Nichols and I were asked to provide a song as background to a mini-movie showing a young couple getting married . . . then driving off into the sunset. It turned out to be more effective than we'd ever imagined."

PHOTO: JOAN LAUREN

"I have a God-shaped hole in the center of my chest and I kept trying to fill it with drugs and people."

Carpenters

PHOTO: JIM McCRARY

"We've Only Just Begun," written by Paul Williams and Roger Nichols, was recorded by the Carpenters for A&M Records in 1970. During its fourteen-week stay on Billboard's Hot 100, it held the #2 position for four weeks and then went on to earn a gold record. It received two Grammy nominations the same year the Carpenters received a Grammy for Best New Artist. Named to the BMI Top 100 Songs, "We've Only Just Begun" has had over five million broadcast performances. The Carpenters' recording was named to the Grammy Hall of Fame in 1998. Paul Williams was inducted into the Songwriters Hall of Fame in 2001 and currently makes his home in Los Angeles, California.

I was born in Omaha, Nebraska, in 1940. My father was a construction worker, so we moved just about every year. I think I must have gone to nine schools by the time I was in the ninth grade. I was sort of a rootless child—was always the new kid and always the littlest kid in school. I didn't know it then, but as a form of self-defense, it probably developed my communication skills at an accelerated rate. So it turned out to be a gift.

Was there any specific time or place in your childhood that had an influence on your music?

As a child, I never thought of music as coming from any place except the radio or the record player. I was twenty-seven years old when I first started writing songs. I was an out-of-work actor and I did it for my own amusement. Back then, music for me came from a time and a place I had missed. It came from the Brill Building, it came from New York, and from the thirties and the forties because that's the music I love. I love Larry Hart, Cole Porter, Rodgers and Hammerstein, all of it music from another era. The music I wanted to be a part of had already been made in a lot of ways. I discovered Sinatra in the fifties when I was in high school. I remember an album, one of the first albums I absolutely loved, called *Manhattan Towers* by Gordon Jenkins. It was this amazing story album of something that was going on at a party in New York. But I really didn't fall in love with contemporary music until probably around the time of the Beatles. The older I get, the more I think that what we write about is the stuff that happens to us in

PHOTO: JIM McCRARY

the first six years of our lives. I think the content of a lot of my songs is what I call emotional anthems, the "Ouch, Mommy" kind of song, meaning "pick me up and love me." What I write about is the tenderness of being held or being left. It goes back to my beginnings and the real influences on me which came from the American lyric masters like Johnny Mercer, Cole Porter, Sammy Cahn, Jimmy Van Heusen, and Johnny Burke. I've always said that I write in American instead of English. If you look at "Evergreen" with a lyric like "Love soft as an easy chair," for example, that's not Keats, it's not Shelley. For me, it's just speaking from a purely emotional and authentic place. And when I write at my most authentic, it's probably when I'm getting dangerously close to Hallmark greeting cards, but it's also the place where I think most people respond.

What part does inspiration play in your songwriting?

I It's largely inspiration. As we walk around, the sum total of all my experiences sort of get added to that songwriter filing cabinet. When I was writing songs for *The Muppet Christmas Carol*, I wrote down "We see the man, not the whole man, just his feet as he comes out of the door. As he passes some little mice they get colder from the wind." Then I read the original *Christmas Carol* by Dickens and everything I could find about Scrooge. I told my inner creative self that I wanted to do this song about Scrooge and this is what we were going to see on the screen. Then I distracted myself and did something entirely different. I started reading a book, a Lawrence Block mystery, as I recall. All of a sudden I put down the book, grabbed a pencil and pad of paper and wrote [sings] "When a cold wind blows it chills you / Chills you to the bone / But there's nothing in nature that freezes your heart / Like years of being alone." It's when I get my mind totally away from what I'm writing that something wonderful rolls out of me, gets pulled out of that writer's filing cabinet. Someone once told me that Henry Mancini had an embroidered pillow in his office which said "You can chase after butterflies all day and never catch one. Stand really still and one will come to you and land on your shoulder." For me, it all gets reduced to that old saying, "Don't squeeze the kitty." If you love the kitty and squeeze it, the kitty will jump out of your lap. Sit there and lightly pet the kitty, it'll stay there all day.

PHOTO: JIM McCRARY

Early on, was there someone you wanted to succeed for?

I think there's a face I put on a lot of people as I pass through life. A few years of Kleinian analysis and you begin to realize it's all the same person. When I was forty-six years old, I left my wife and kids for a twenty-two-year-old psych major who was "the one." I mean she was absolutely the one. She was the first person who dared to reflect the truth back to me and said, "You're an alcoholic and an addict and you're gonna die if you don't get help, and I won't be around to watch you do that." So she was the first person I tried to get sober for. But it didn't work. And when she left I remember thinking "I can't live without this person." Then after some time, I would see her around, you know, casually, and I realized that in fact she wasn't "the one" I was remembering at all. And so I began to realize that there's this imagined face, the "face" of the one who can fix you that exists in all of our minds. And we put that face on different people who pass through our lives and for a while it fits, and then they're gone. But somewhere along the line I realized that what I was missing was a relationship with God. I have a God-shaped hole in the center of my chest and I kept trying to fill it with drugs and people. So for me, what's important is to maintain a spiritual life. I believe that the people who pass through your life on whom you try to fit that "face" all leave something of themselves behind.

PHOTO: JIM McCRARY

When I started writing again about five years ago, I wrote a song with Jon Vezner called "You're Gone" which says "And the good news is I'm better for the time we spent together / And the bad news is you're gone." I think we're all soul catchers, if I can use that expression. I think as people pass through our lives we catch bits and pieces of their wisdom, their affection, their whatever that fits in our lives and stays with us. Maybe that's what builds us into better people as time passes. So in the end you become a kind of compilation. Maybe recognizing that you become a receptacle and embracing that is one of the great spiritual tools offered to us. But the biggest change in my life at this point is that I see every day as a blessing and that's been the greatest gift of the last twelve years.

Was there a specific time when you felt you had made it?

What success I've had in my career arrived in kind of a flurry and then sort of dribbled down to a level where it's supposed to be. I had so little consciousness of my life in my thirties. I just thought I was six feet tall and bulletproof and it was forever. A lot of my early success was destructive for me. I think I became better at showing off than showing up. The part of me that became an entertainer and a "celebrity" or "television personality" began to chisel away at the writer part of me. Celebrity actually got between me and the writer. At its most basic level, part of writing is the ability to observe without being observed. I think I did some great work during those early years, but I also wasted a lot of time. Even so, those years would really be wasted now if I didn't use them in my life today, every day. What's good about my life now is that I think I've never felt more useful. A lot of it is about my openness, about my recovery and talking about the disease of alcoholism, drug abuse, and the hope of recovery.

The songwriter who needs anonymity and the actor who needs to be seen would appear to be opposing forces.

Exactly, but it makes for a great life drama. When I got out of high school I was four foot six inches tall and looked nine years old. I was eight inches shorter than I am now. Imagine, I went to Hollywood and said I want to be an actor. I was impossible to cast. I looked like a kid until you put me next to a real kid, then I just looked like a kid with a hangover. It seems that on a lot of levels I chose the most difficult path in the world. The fact is that I found work in small films and then in major films. I got to the point where I began to feed myself, began to nurture myself, which in turn allowed me room to find my creative expression in songwriting. Initially, I did it for my own amusement. I had this creative energy that needed to be expressed and so it just began. And it was a series of wonderful accidents that took me to A&M Records and Roger Nichols, my writing partner. Most of my life, it's like I've been redirected by bumping into walls or doors that won't open and then a "no" turns into a "yes" that's bigger. I think the big change for me was I finally quit fighting who I am as a writer.

Is there anyone you wished you could have met over the years or talked to?

I don't know why Stan Laurel comes to mind, but he does. It just kills me that Stan Laurel was living down there in Santa Monica and I didn't get to talk with him or for that matter, with Ira Gershwin, when he was still with us. Yet by the same token, I remember having dinner at Groucho Marx's house and not having any brilliant questions for Groucho. I don't know what I would have asked Ira Gershwin, I don't know that we would have had a meaningful conversation. One of those moments in life I'll always remember was at A&M studios where I once waited for over an hour, outside by the coffee machine, because Johnny Mercer was mixing something in one of the studios. I could have gone and knocked on the door, but I just wanted to sort of "magically" run into Johnny Mercer. Eventually, Mercer came out to get a cup of coffee and I said "Hi, Mr. Mercer. My name is Paul Williams and it's an honor to meet you." All he said was, "Nice to meet you," shook my hand and went back into the mix room. And I stood there and just went "Brrrrrrr." Maybe it was a minute later he stuck his head out of the door and said "'What I've got they used to call the blues' [from 'Rainy Days and Mondays'], that Paul Williams?" And I said in a child's voice, "Yes, sir," and he came over and we talked. As it turned out, we had nothing much to say to each other except that he was very complimentary. It was one of those great instances when I got that ego satisfaction just for a moment. But even if we'd had more time together, I don't know what I would have asked him. What do you ask another writer? Through the years I wish I had told some people how much I love them, how much I love their work. I never met Don McLean, but in every interview I've ever done where they ask what I wish I had written, I start off with "Vincent."

Graham's [Graham Nash] song "Simple Man" with "I just want to hold you / I don't want to hold you down" is something I always mention, something I wish I had written. Also "I need you more than want you and I want you for all time" from Jimmy Webb's "Wichita Lineman." They're amazing lines but I wouldn't have anything to say to Jimmy or to Graham or to Don McLean about that. It's usually disappointing to talk to a writer you really love because writers aren't necessarily great conversationalists.

Was there anyone who ever tried to talk you out of following your dreams?

For me, more than I didn't have the talent, what I always got was, "Let's be realistic about your physical limitations to go be an actor" or "Don't you want to get an education?" My older brother once made an appointment for me with the Department of Employment with Special Services which got jobs for people who are handicapped or something. I was really furious with him. Occasionally, I get asked for advice by people who want to become songwriters, singers, or actors, but especially songwriters. And my line to them is always the same: If you have a real talent smoldering away in your chest, I don't believe that talent was put there for you to suffer. I think it was put there for you to use. Ignore the bastards who tell you you can't do it. Sometimes I add as an addendum to get an education, but frankly, I don't really mean it. If you're a writer, go write. If you're a singer, go find a band, collaborate, get into a garage band, go sing in bars. I think if I had to make the choice of being thirty and hungry and having pursued my dreams with nothing coming of it, or with being thirty, doing well and sitting in a bank working somewhere and never having tried, I'd go for poor, hungry, and thirty. Because at least you know you've done it, at least you know you've tried. I say be courageous.

Disc Two
Track 13

Peter Yarrow on
"Puff (The Magic Dragon)"

Puff (The Magic Dragon)

Peter Yarrow and Leonard Lipton

Puff the magic dragon lived by the sea
And frolicked in the autumn mist in a land called Honalee.
Little Jackie Paper loved that rascal Puff
and brought him strings and sealing wax and other fancy stuff.

Chorus:

Puff the magic dragon lived by the sea
And frolicked in the autumn mist in a land called Honalee.
Puff the magic dragon lived by the sea
And frolicked in the autumn mist in a land called Honalee.

Together they would travel on a boat with billowed sail
Jackie kept a lookout perched on Puff's gigantic tail.
Noble kings and princes would bow whene'er they came.
Pirate ships would low'r their flags when Puff roared out his name.

Chorus:

A dragon lives forever, but not so little boys.
Painted wings and giants' rings make way for other toys.
One gray night it happened, Jackie Paper came no more,
And Puff that mighty dragon, he ceased his fearless roar.

His head was bent in sorrow, green tears fell like rain.
Puff no longer went to play along the Cherry Lane.
Without his lifelong friend, Puff could not be brave,
So Puff that mighty dragon sadly slipped into his cave. Oh!

Chapter 25

Peter Yarrow

PHOTO: ROBERT CORWIN

Puff, the Magic Dragon

Puff, the magic dragon lived by the sea
And frolicked in the autumn mist in a land called Honah Lee
Little Jackie Paper loved that rascal Puff
And brought him strings and sealing wax
And other fancy stuff

Together they would travel on a boat with billowed sail
Jackie kept a lookout perched on Puff's gigantic tail
Noble kings + Princes would bow when'ere they came
Pirate ships would lower their flags when Puff roared out
his name

A dragon lives forever — but not so little girls and boys
Painted wings and giants' rings make way for other toys
One gray night it happened, Jackie Paper came no more
And Puff that mighty dragon, he ceased his fearless roar

His head was bent in sorrow. Green scales fell like rain.
Puff no longer went to play along the cherry lane
Without his life-long friend, Puff could not be brave
So Puff that mighty dragon, sadly slipped into
his cave

A/Z 5/95

196

"Puff is really about the innocence of childhood lost and in that song there is a bittersweet tone that is characteristic of a lot of the songs I've written."

"My advice to aspiring writers is to be part of a community of songwriters; nurture each other, validate each other, and encourage each other to write from the heart."

Peter, Paul, and Mary

PHOTO: ©EBET ROBERTS/
CHANSLEY ENTERTAINMENT ARCHIVES

"Puff, the Magic Dragon," written by Peter Yarrow and Lenny Lipton, was first recorded by Peter, Paul, and Mary for Warner Bros. Records in 1963. Climbing Billboard's Top 40 *for eleven weeks, it peaked at the #2 position and earned the #1 spot on* Billboard's Middle-Road Singles *chart (easy listening). "Puff, the Magic Dragon" received a Grammy nomination for Best Recording for Children and later became the subject of three animated television specials, which earned Peter Yarrow an Emmy nomination. Peter Yarrow lives in New York City.*

I was born in New York City on May 31, 1938, which means I was a teenager in the fifties. Because of my background and my family's perspective, I was keenly aware of the McCarthy era and how it was part of the fault line of the competing perspectives within our country. The circumstances were not terribly dissimilar from the dichotomy that exists today. While the dominant part of our society was focused on wealth, power, and social status, the other part was focused on a new and evolving perspective relating to issues of social justice, fairness, and a way of living together compassionately and respectfully—both as individuals and as a society.

I went to high school between 1951 and 1955, which, in some circles, is still referred to as "scoundrel time," (I'm referring to Samuel Johnson's quote, "Patriotism is the last refuge of a scoundrel"). The era of Senator Joe McCarthy is sometimes referred to as scoundrel time because his blacklist ushered in one of the darkest periods in American history, in terms of dealing with a pernicious internal threat to the foundations of our democracy. Political issues and social justice issues in that period were all very starkly defined.

Do you think the fifties set the stage for the kind of culture shock we experienced in the sixties?

The sixties, the period following that dark era, witnessed a reversal of the fifties pendulum sweep in

PHOTO COURTESY OF SHOWTIME MUSIC
ARCHIVES (TORONTO)

some ways, and signaled the beginning of the kind of consciousness that celebrated the importance of each individual's identity and perspective. It was the emergence of a concept of a society in which people thought for themselves, rather than marching to blind patriotism's drummer. Patriotism, yes. Blind patriotism, no! To me, the most important evolution of the sixties emerged in the context of the Civil Rights movement. There was a parallel evolution of people's points of view in the sixties that was embodied by the "flower children" or hippies, and their music was a proactive symbol and expression of their belief system. To me, in retrospect, this so-called hippie counterculture, although colorful and loving, did not affirm an approach to life, a way of living that took responsibility for addressing the dilemmas of the world or precipitated a search for their solutions. The flower children, frequently absorbed in "dropping out," in large part embraced an important but fairly narrow perspective—that of keeping one's private house in order and being a good individual—but it neglected to address the role of citizens in confronting larger, crucial world-threatening issues.

At the time, the sixties generation thought it was making a good point.

In my opinion, dropping out, in that sense, was counterproductive. Being good, being caring and loving are all well and good but having a larger sense of social responsibility is, to me, a necessary part of life. A humanistic and proactive view of one's participation in world events was certainly needed then, but is needed now more than ever.

Peter, Paul, and Mary, 1960s

Was your musical contribution intended to serve these greater goals?

Yes, and that's the main reason I chose this career. Of course, I love the music, but I never would've chosen it as a career except for my early awareness of its remarkable capacity to reach beyond verbal and logical considerations. It can influence people's hearts in such a way that they can connect one to another and build community together. I know that the word "community" sounds somewhat fuzzy and prosaic, but what I mean by community is to tangibly let human beings sense that they are connected to one another, for better or worse, and invested in each other's lives. Having awakened that sense of connectivity, that musical experience can become an engine of mutual recognition and empowerment—one that allows people to advance positive political efforts and inspire greater social awareness.

Do you have an example of what you're describing?

As a senior, I was offered an undergraduate instructorship at Cornell University teaching English 355-356, Folk Music and Folk Ballads, which was popularly called "Romp 'n' Stomp." In those days, people would take this "gut" course primarily to raise their grade point average. On Saturday, instead of having a class per se, we'd just have a sing-along. So instead of going to the student union at ten A.M., traditionally called "ten o'clock dead hour," they'd come to this class. First,

PHOTO COURTESY OF SHOWTIME MUSIC ARCHIVES (TORONTO)/PICTORIAL PRESS

it was in the hundreds, and not long after, over a thousand students would be spilling out into the hall. This opportunity, and I acknowledge its larger implications for my later life's work, turned Saturdays at Cornell into a student-faculty hootenanny of sorts.

Was your thinking at that time along the lines of that of Woody Guthrie and Pete Seeger's theory that while music is entertaining, it can also be an instrument of social awakening and change?

Yes, but let me bring this whole story to a focus. On those Saturdays in "Romp 'n' Stomp," I saw a real transformation; students sang with such passion, with such openness, such heart, that the music clearly helped transcend all the artificial boundaries that,

199

in Cornell of the late fifties, separated many students from their own sensitivity and humanity. In a very innocent way, the simple act of singing a song cut through logical preconceptions, and went straight to their hearts. The students came together in song, despite their adversity to breaking down the barriers of a very serious and, to some, painful, social hierarchy. After I experienced that "miracle on the quad," I realized that I wanted to go out and be engaged in this kind of community-building process; breaking down barriers and reaching people's hearts through music

Where did that take you next?

When I graduated from Cornell, I went straight to Greenwich Village and started performing for tips when the hat was passed at the Café Wha? on MacDougal Street. I carried with me the ethos of songwriters such as the Weavers who saw music as a tool to raise consciousness and unite people in an effort to make the world a fairer, more just and caring place. Of course, their careers, after an explosion of top-of-the-charts hits like "Goodnight, Irene" and "Tzena, Tzena, Tzena," were for all intents and purposes destroyed by Senator Joe McCarthy's blacklist which effectively eliminated the playing of their records on the radio, their ability to go on TV, and the willingness of clubs to book them. It's no coincidence that when Peter, Paul, and Mary emerged in a somewhat more tolerant time, our first songs included "If I Had a Hammer" and "Where Have All the Flowers Gone?" Both these songs were written by members of the Weavers; Pete Seeger wrote "Flowers" and he and Lee Hays wrote "If I Had a Hammer."

What are your current commitments?

These days, my major non–Peter, Paul, and Mary commitment is to a project and charitable organization that I founded in 1999 called Operation Respect which seeks to change the culture of classrooms and schools by shifting educational emphasis so that

Peter, Paul, and Mary
Newport Jazz Festival, 1960s

PHOTO: MICHAEL OCHS ARCHIVES.COM

students' social and emotional development is given the same kind of priority and attention as their academic progress. There's a song called "Don't Laugh at Me," written by Steve Seskin and Alan Shamblin, that has become the anthem of a movement that endeavors to create respectful, caring, non-bullying, and emotionally safe environments for children in schools, summer camps, boys and girls clubs, et cetera. The song "Don't Laugh at Me" is to this movement what "Blowing in the Wind," "If I Had a Hammer," and "We Shall Overcome" were to the Civil Rights movement and other movements that followed. So, by linking a song to social change, I'm simply continuing on the same path that I traveled when I first graduated from college. Effectively, I'm now working as part of a national movement supported by virtually all the major educational organizations of America and over a hundred members of the Congress and the Senate. Together, we are attempting to do something fundamental to achieve what we tried to accomplish in the sixties, seventies, eighties, and nineties. Ultimately, we need to provide children with the social and emotional tools that will lead to their respecting one another as they accept and embrace each other's differences, and learn how to resolve their conflicts nonviolently. Kids must also start performing service to their community very early, to "walk the walk," as early as first grade. If these Character Education tools are provided for them, then we stand a much better chance of not having to suffer the horrors of Columbine, Paducah, Springfield, and Santee, again and again. We will not have to helplessly watch as the seeds of racism and warfare are planted for successive generations—and we will not have to watch as arrogance and blindness to other people's and countries' excruciating needs fan the flames of hatred and terrorism.

In terms of songwriting, is there anyone who was a major influence on your work whom you would have liked to have discussed some of these issues with but never had a chance?

Well, I think my influences are reflected in the thematic songs I've written like "Day Is Done," "Light One Candle," "River of

Jordan," and "Weave Me the Sunshine." They all, to one degree or another, have a certain balance and perspective, which include bits of the struggle combined with our hopes and dreams. For instance, if you look at "Puff, the Magic Dragon," which I wrote with Leonard Lipton, the portion to me that ultimately grabs me is not just the adventure of meeting and playing with dragon, but the idea of the dragon living forever "but not so little girls and boys." Puff is really about the innocence of childhood lost and in that song there is a bittersweet tone that is characteristic of a lot of the songs I've written. So to answer your question, it was in that tradition in folk music, that sense of living real life, experiencing it as struggle and a joy, and telling the truth about it, that I found my teacher. I love that aspect of folk music. It's not written for the bucks, and way back the roots music set the stage for that kind of songwriting today.

How do you channel these larger issues into the constraints of lyric writing?

It's interesting because I think anyone who writes, may, without conscious intent, somehow reflect or shape the world around him or herself. This can emerge from a special kind of partnership between the writer or singer and the listener. Such a partnership is apparent, for example, in a song I called "Moments of the Soft Persuasion." This is a pretty nonlinear song describing the awakening to one's own spirituality. The listener needs to engage with the writer to decide what the song means. I tried, as others had before me, to ask for a much deeper participation than can be elicited from just the simple sharing of direct information. You can see the modeling of real engagement in the writing of Bob Dylan. Take the lyric phrase, "The answer, my friend, is blowing in the wind." What does that mean? Nobody knows except what it means to you. In a way, it doesn't matter what his intent was; it's all about sharing the song and exploring its meaning. That partnership between performer and listener can move and empower an audience or a listener to come to terms with his or her own beliefs or point of view. In a way, this partnership was an important part of the evolution of the music of the sixties and the national cultural shift, as I see it. Poetry has always had this quality, but it was folk music in the sixties that exemplified this writer-listener empowering partnership.

What advice would you care to give to aspiring young writers?

I do believe the current music business and the fast food business have both successfully learned to market a daily massive dose of non-nutritional product. There are some notable exceptions like Alanis Morissette and Fiona Apple but these are atypical. There's a place for being playful, a place for the exchange of la-la land signals. But it's dangerous when it's all about dollars, when success hinges on marketing rather than talent, and people's hearts and intellects are not engaged. Consequently, because of my perspective on the role music can play in society, my advice to aspiring writers is to be a part of a community of songwriters; nurture each other, validate each other, and encourage each other to write from the heart.

Manuscript Originals

Manuscript Originals

Manuscript Originals was created in 1993 by Graham Nash and several music industry associates to honor and commemorate the classic songs of our times in the form of museum-quality, limited-edition handwritten lyrics rendered by one of the song's original composers. These limited-edition pieces are available through the Neiman Marcus stores, art galleries, and other exclusive venues throughout the country.

For further information regarding Manuscript Originals and our products:
Please contact 1-800-9-LYRICS (1-800-959-7427) or visit our Web site at www.oursong.com.